When Trauma Survivors Return to Work

Understanding Emotional Recovery

A Handbook for Managers and Co-Workers

Barbara Barski-Carrow

UNIVERSITY PRESS OF AMERICA,® INC.

Lanham • Boulder • New York • Toronto • Plymouth, UK

Copyright © 2010 by
University Press of America,® Inc.
4501 Forbes Boulevard
Suite 200
Lanham, Maryland 20706
UPA Acquisitions Department (301) 459-3366

Estover Road
Plymouth PL6 7PY
United Kingdom

Library of Congress Control Number: 2009942755
ISBN: 978-0-7618-5030-4 (paperback : alk. paper)
eISBN: 978-0-7618-5031-1

♾ ™ The paper used in this publication meets the minimum
requirements of American National Standard for Information
Sciences—Permanence of Paper for Printed Library Materials,
ANSI Z39.48-1992

For my husband, Milton

Contents

PART III. SOME SPECIAL CIRCUMSTANCES

Acknowledgments

I am grateful to many people who have helped me navigate this road of authorship, those who continue to support my research and work. First of all, my agent Diane Nine has not only helped me with the fine points of writing and structure, but also her sense of humor and integrity. Her skill grounded me in this project and she was always available to talk to me about my concerns. My associate editor, Brooke Bascietto, demanded from me a commitment to excellence, for which I am grateful. She also helped me navigate this road with creative ease. Samantha M. Kirk, my acquisitions editor, was available to speak with me on questions relative to the process. To her I am appreciative.

My all inspiring friend, Helen Thomas, provided frequent conversations that were invaluable to me on this journey.

I am deeply indebted to Dr. Louis Savary and Dr. Patricia Berne, who have helped me hold the vision for my book and continued to encourage me with patience and a guiding hand. This book would not have materialized without them. I cherish their professional support and their friendship. Lou studied the complete manuscript and spent many hours editing, reviewing and rearranging the text for publication. His insights and suggestions helped the book become a whole. Pat's contribution to the insight of survivors and their psychological dynamics greatly enhanced the overall content of the book.

Dr. Dory Hollander is a savvy and intuitive advisor and friend, who provided a wealth of wisdom and encouragement. Dr. Constance Condrell, a friend and mentor has taught me to keep an open mind and always examine all alternatives.

Over the years, as the manuscript went through its genesis and gestation, many friends and colleagues have helped bring it to life. My dearest and best friend, Mary C. McDonnell, continued to encourage me and love me throughout this project always uplifting my spirits and keeping my thoughts focused on the result I wanted to accomplish. Mary has been, and remains, my partner in creativity.

Among these wonderful and constant friends is Dr. Phyllis O'Callaghan whose voice continued over many lunches to resonate throughout all of my research. She encouraged me when the road got rough and I got weary, and she helped me to realize the finished product. Also, Dr. Elizabeth (Betty) Duke served as a mentor and role model for excellence, knowledge and learn-ing--there is none better. Betty has been an inspiration to me throughout my career and professional growth.

I would like to recognize Dr. Harold Stubblefield, professor, scholar and friend. He believed in my "golden nugget" and guided me with wise feed-back as I developed my research. Other faculty members at Virginia Tech (Virginia Polytechnic Institute and State University) who played a role in my research experience are Dr. Jerry Cline, Dr. Ronald McKeen, Dr. Marcie Boucouvalas and Dr. Gabriella Belli.

I would also like to thank Dr. Robert Neimeyer, a colleague, friend and mentor who supported my research and work. After Bob heard me speak at a conference, he paid me the greatest compliment by referring to my research and using my work in his lectures. His steady hand and illuminating ideas were always valuable to me in collaborating with him on issues relative to the next phase of working with trauma and grief in the workplace.

I am grateful to my colleagues at the Department of Health and Human Services (HHS) in Washington, DC a heartfelt thank you for their commit-ment to my research. All the participants who were interviewed and partici-pated in the Study Circles helped me develop an educational model in the workplace like no other. The dimensions of learning were enormous with feedback from both employees and managers on how their behavior changed after participating in the Study Circles. My supervisor, Barbara Aulenbach, is a wonderful friend, mentor and partner in the process. She provided advice, friendship and love of wanting to make a difference in people's lives. She whole-heartedly supported my work in creating a more compassionate and enlighten workplace environment for traumatized workers.

Friends in Virgin Gorda (British Virgin Islands) were always there to sup-port me when I wanted to take a break from writing. Dr. Jeanne Dalton and Rita Kallman shared many cups of coffee and lunches with me and Pat and Nelson Tyler read the final manuscript offering their support and encourage-ment.

My colleagues at ADEC (Association for Death Education and Counsel-ing) gathered at many conferences and wanted to know the progress of my book and offered suggestions and support. I would like to recognize Dr. Janice Winchester Nadeau who had time to meet with me for lunch to discuss my book. She always returned a phone call no matter where she was in the world. I am thankful to Thomas Attig, whose unique approach to storytelling helped me to understand my work and make application in my writing. Dr. J. Shep Jeffreys model of workplace grief showed me another way of looking at workplace interactions. Linda Goldman, is a friend and colleague whose conversations on her work with children and grief helped me understand this importance application to my model.

I would like to thank The Study Circle Resource Center in Pomfret, Connecticut—their help in finding whatever I needed for my research along with the opportunity to meet and participate in the Study Circle Workshop offered immense growth and understanding to the process.

Spiritually one cannot embark on a project like this without the guidance from a friend or pastor. One of the people in this endeavor was Deacon Jim Purks of Georgia. Jim's experience and work at the White House and with Habitat for Humanity brought a serene, calm approach to understanding the events of the universe. Our conversations relative to grief, healing and trauma lifted my spirits many times in this writing. The other person is my partner in perseverance and hope: Dr. Barbara Dane, a gifted therapist, writer, scholar and spiritual friend, she always called at the right time and offered nutrition to my soul and helped me to believe in my research and trust the universe.

To many of my friends along the way I want to thank them for their support and friendship who have heard my lectures and always wanted to know more about my research: Edward Badaloto, Marti Barrett, Virginia Bau, Jane Brown, Louise Betterman, Charles and Linda Cassell, Maryann Dera, Helen Dildy, Dr. Marian Egge, Patricia Froggett, Louise Frohling, Susan Hamilton, Peter Paul Jodoin, Dr. Elizabeth Johns, Jackie LaMere, Rosalie LaMonica, Elfie Lindquist, Ginnie McPeak, Dr. Karen McWilliams, Dr. Jacqueline Magness, Helene Markoff, Paul O'Leary, Niki Pearson, John Potocki, Dr. Martha Redstrom Plourd, Dr. Elizabeth Roslewicz, Leslie Sorg Ramsay, Claudia Urban, and Renee Younes.

Also, my friend in London, England, David Charles-Edwards, who, through our emails and writings, has researched work on workplace grief. I would like to give a genuine thank you for his collaborations. To Jennifer Brengle and Edward Kowalczyk who kept my home running smoothly while I was writing and compiling the manuscript. I am truly grateful for their friendship and support. Kevin Spence, to whom I would like to thank for his keen eye and articulate manner, gave me excellent help and feedback on the final manuscript. His tireless efforts I applaud. I am grateful to Mary Founds for her friendship and support along with her wizardry with a computer. She was there right to the end giving me the support I needed to finish this process.

MY FAMILY

To my parents, Michael and Catherine for their love and support for my educational and life goals, especially my mother whose presence and voice I enjoy everyday. She helped me believe I could accomplish whatever I set out to do in my life. My father, his spirit is with me everyday—his gifts to me are too numerous to mention. I also want to thank my brother Michael and sister-in-law Bernadette and niece Lydia for their support, interest and encouragement.

To my extended family, here is where I have been blessed—the two cheerleaders who were with me every step of the way were my uncle Dr. Walter Novelli and my Aunt Loretta (Novelli)-Fischetti. Their spirit of love, support and encouragement has shaped my life. To my extended family and all my aunts and uncles and cousins who have been a strength for me. I thank them.

At last, my husband, Milton. I dedicate my book to him. I have been blessed with a unique individual, who not only is gifted in his strength and love for me, but in his outlook, experience and world view of life. His steady and predictable hand offers consistent love, support and trust in the visions that we hold in our life.

Introduction

As adults, most of us spend more time on the job than we do in any other setting or activity, typically finding in the workplace a sense of connection, structure, meaning and identity that evolves across our lifetime. More tragically, most of us will also know—often more than once—the traumatic disruption of our worlds that results from the death of loved ones, serious illness in oneself or in the family, a tragic accident, victimization by crime, unanticipated divorce, and other losses that shake our foundations and leave us feeling dazed and distant from other people who have not known such adversity. Barbara Barski-Carrow's book, *When Trauma Survivors Return to Work*, is about what happens when these two worlds, the world of work and the world of personal trauma, collide. More important, it is a book about what to do about it, dispensing practical guidance for every manager and co-worker who ever wonders how to respond to a traumatized employee who seeks to re-enter the workplace after a life-altering adverse event. And ultimately, that readership includes nearly all of us.

As a psychologist who specializes in research and treatment with people who have experienced profound bereavement and loss, I am aware of the many resources for professional psychotherapists who seek to help their clients deal with traumatic life experiences, what Barski-Carrow calls *TLEs*. I am also aware of the almost equally numerous books and programs for people negotiating this traumatic terrain, at least in its common forms, as they deal with their personal losses through death, divorce and disease. But what has been almost entirely missing—until now—is a resource for those who share the workplace with colleagues who are struggling with the aftermath of these experiences, that will help us find the right words, actions and policies to reintegrate the TLE employee back into the community of the workplace, and promote his or her resumption of meaningful activities that benefit not only the employee, but also the organization of which he or she is a part. Barski-Carrow's readable, down-to-earth advice fills this gap, using the stories of many employees and managers facing the challenge of reintegration to convey flexible principles and procedures for helping restore the TLE employee's sense of safety and productivity upon return to the work setting.

At the heart of Barski-Carrow's advice is the Study Circle, an innovative application of adult learning methods, in which a small group of people—in this case employees and managers—get together for a few sessions to discuss deeply and personally, but with guidance provided by contemporary psychological research, what the TLE employee needs, and how those who work with him or her can help provide it. Although Barski-Carrow is explicit in distinguishing between the role of manager or co-worker on the one hand and psychotherapist or counselor on the other, she nonetheless believes, rightly, that there is much that a traumatized worker's colleagues can do to provide a secure, welcoming environment in which healing can occur, offering a place where the employee's story can be heard with compassion, and where work tasks can be adjusted and shared so as to promote her or his successful adaptation. In this sense, I found the book to be among the most *empowering* of any I have read, sensitively leading participants in the TLE employee's work life from a position of awkward silence or embarrassment to a position of empathic competence in a trying circumstance. And for managers concerned with the "bottom line," the value of drawing on Barski-Carrow's advice to help retain valued employees and build group morale rather than suffer a further loss of both is substantial, whatever the work setting, large or small.

Why should you, as a busy manager or employee, take time to read this book? Simply stated, because you need it. As any one of us can attest, life is filled with challenges, some of them catastrophic. And when these challenges arrive on the doorsteps of those with whom we work—as they will—we will benefit immensely from the practical, engaging and insightful perspective and procedures imparted in these pages. Your colleagues and supervisors will thank you for it with their words and actions, as will those TLE employees whose loyalty and commitment you will have cemented by your skillful response to some of their lives' darkest moments. In this book, you will find a good companion in this effort.

> Robert A. Neimeyer, PhD
> Editor, *Death Studies* and
> Author, *Lessons of Loss: A Guide to Coping*

Part I

UNDERSTANDING THE TRAUMATIC LIFE EXPERIENCE (TLE)

Chapter One

Why I Wrote This Book

Traumatic Life Experiences in one form or another have always been and will always be with us. Authors, poets and playwrights have used themes of trauma and loss as grist for their creative works. From their stories and from our own experience we know that individuals who survive and overcome trauma often achieve a transcending perspective on themselves. For those who allow trauma to defeat them, life remains a complicated and painful struggle. Willy Loman, the tragic figure in Arthur Miller's "Death of a Salesman," was one of those who gave up. Plagued by anger, rejection and depression caused by a trauma related to the workplace, he seemed unable to recover. Luckily, most traumatized workers, unlike Willy, seem to make it back as survivors.

I, myself, am one of these survivors. While an employee and manager for many years in the federal offices of the Department of Health and Human Services, I encountered many returning trauma survivors and heard the sad stories of many more. At the university, I majored in communication arts, and so had some small advantage over other managers who seemed to be in over their heads when it came to communicating with trauma survivors at work. But I too was baffled at how to facilitate re-entry for them. Seeing so many confused managers—myself included—inspired me in my doctoral work in adult education to find practical ways to educate managers and co-workers about understanding the emotional recovery from trauma, so they could help, not hinder, that process in the workplace. The reason I wrote this book is to show what I discovered in my research—and to help myself become a better manager.

What got me started was a sad story about a thoughtless manager that I heard first hand from Diane, a friend of mine from college days.

Diane, an executive with a software company, had been walking down the hall to her weekly staff meeting when her secretary rushed up to her with a phone message that said, "Urgent!!! Call Home." A few moments later, Diane learned that her three-year-old daughter Megan had been hit by a car near the school playground and had been taken to the hospital. Diane ran to her car and headed for the hospital. On her way, she called her husband on her cell phone, who set out for the hospital immediately.

At the hospital, the doctor told Diane her daughter was seriously hurt and needed emergency surgery. She called her office to speak with her boss. To him, she explained her situation and said her daughter was going to undergo surgery that evening, and asked for "emergency leave." Insensitive to her needs, the boss reminded her of the projects that were due and the importance of the budget report that needed her revisions. He added that it was urgent that he talk with her about some personnel decisions that had to be made by the close of business that day. She pointed out that her assistant could handle all those items, but her boss seemed insistent that she be in contact with him first thing in the morning. He also told her he might call her on her cell phone later that day to clear up any difficult items. Not expecting this unsympathetic response, she simply said she would get back to him.

Neither Diane nor her husband had any family living in the area, as they had recently re-located from the Midwest and were just getting settled. Later that day, when she reached her mother and asked for assistance, it turned out her mother, recuperating from an operation, could not come for two weeks. Diane chose to be with her daughter, and remain at her side. She decided she would simply take the time off from work and deal with the consequences of her decision when she returned. She then phoned her assistant at work and made arrangements to talk with her after her daughter's surgery the next day. The following week she remained with her daughter and awaited her mother's arrival.

When a traumatic event, such as happened to Diane, occurs to someone in the workplace, it can usually upset not only the employee herself but also her managers and co-workers. Often, when returning employees who face traumatic life experiences are senior managers like Diane, they have so many demands on their work schedules that it is very hard to pass on responsibilities to others. So, while they are away from the office, urgent responsibilities pile up creating more stress on top of the traumatic life experience. When higher managers like Diane's boss are overly focused on getting the job done, they can easily forget that traumatized employees are also fragile human beings. This is the lack of understanding Diane experienced when talking with him the day of her daughter's accident and when she returned to work.

THE COST TO BUSINESS OF TRAUMATIC LIFE EXPERIENCES

Today, traumatic life experiences happen to workers more often than ever before. Statistics show that on a list of productivity-loss issues, following an employee illness, the category of traumatic life experiences that occur at work or elsewhere are the largest category of reasons for employee absence. Also noted would be the lack of productivity when such traumatized employees return to the workplace. And the reason for this loss is not always simply the returning TLE employee. Managers by the quality of their response to the returning employee may exert a strong influence on the staff's productivity for good or ill.

While some trauma survivors manage to pull themselves up by their own bootstraps, most make it back only with the continued support of others. This support centers on trauma victims re-establishing connections with their public and private worlds. I will show very simply how managers and co-workers can provide such helpful support in the workplace.

My focus is on employees returning to the workplace after experiencing a traumatic life experience (TLE), a term I coined after a number of years of observing people trying to cope with traumas in their lives. I am suggesting a basic yet powerful educational experience for managers who supervise such traumatized employees returning to the workplace after being away for a period of time.

My approach is to bring a well-tested adult educational method into the workplace where managers and co-workers can learn in a short time the basic stages in the process of emotional recovery from most kinds of single-event traumatic experiences. This educational intervention is called the Study Circle, and its theme in this context is *understanding the emotional recovery from trauma* and how managers and co-workers can cooperate with and foster this process in their ordinary interactions with a returning TLE employee. This book aims to provide a way of getting some of that Study Circle experience.

In these pages, I am not going to spend a lot of time analyzing and comparing types of traumatic experiences and therapeutic methods, since it makes no sense to expect managers to become psychologists and make diagnoses of emotional problems. I am not asking or expecting managers to serve as therapists in the workplace but rather to learn how to support professional therapeutic counseling by providing an appropriate workplace environment that will not hinder but promote the healing and emotional recovery process.

TLE individuals like Diane and many others are entitled to return to a full and productive life. They should be able in their own time to re-enter the workforce easily and go forward with as little resistance as possible. However, before them lies a difficult road to recovery and an even more difficult road to full productivity as employees. With proper education and coaching, managers and co-workers can make the journey easier for them.

According to David M. Noer (1993) in his book *Healing the Wounds: Overcoming the trauma of layoffs and revitalizing downsized organizations* traumatic experiences have caused employees to lose their sense of self, their sense of confidence, and their ability to function as before. He writes of the experiences of survivors of the NASA space shuttle disaster:

> After the space shuttle Challenger disaster, the thousands of people who had worked in the shuttle program felt like disaster survivors. Descriptions of the symptoms experienced by these survivors . . . provide an example of survivor symptom similarity. Shortly after the disaster, observers said that shuttle survivors experienced guilt, anxiety, and fear with the full intensity of these feelings yet to be dealt with because of their denial (p. 39).[1]

It is critical for the recovery of survivors who have experienced trauma to renew connections with their co-workers and those people who compose their work world. They need to re-establish the interpersonal elements that were damaged by the traumatic experience. This includes such basic human capabilities as trust, autonomy, initiative, competence, identity and intimacy. Just as these capabilities were formed in earlier relationships with people, they were likely distorted or even destroyed by the traumatic experience. Consequently, they may need to be re-formed and re-created when a traumatized individual returns to the workplace, depending on the type and intensity of the trauma.

One does not need to be an expert to realize that government agencies as well as organizations in the private sector "suffer" when any of their employees are traumatized either within the organization by workplace violence or outside the organization, by personal trauma. The corporate suffering can easily be observed and measured in overall morale problems and lower productivity, caused not only by traumatized employees but also by the inability of managers and co-workers to effectively deal with those employees when they return to their jobs. Traumatized employees cost organizations the interruption of business, increased absences, low morale and low productivity. Reported in an article in the *LRP Publications Federal Human Resources Week Magazine,* the National Safe Workplace Institute estimated that the costs to businesses in the United States from workplace violence alone exceed $4.2 billion annually.

The business community is naturally concerned about preventing these kinds of incidents from continually happening. Much has been written about *prevention* of workplace violence and trauma, namely, how to observe and report warning signs of potential outbursts. Michael Mantell's (1994) book *Ticking Bombs: Diffusing Violence in the Workplace* is a good example of this. But prevention of trauma and recovery from it are two different matters.

Whenever traumas can be prevented, it is of course the best solution. But the fact is that, no matter how much we try to prevent them, traumatic events do happen inside and outside the workplace. And after they happen, we must deal with them, relationships must be re-established, and work must go on.

What has not been available before now is a compassionate and effective way for managers and co-workers to deal with the *aftermath of traumatic events*, specifically how to treat returning employees who have had a traumatic life experience, whether in the workplace or elsewhere. The emotional toll on these returning employees in trying to grieve their traumatic losses and put their lives back together again is resulting in extended absenteeism, people leaving work early, faulty workmanship and projects not being completed. We have only to recall the terrorist attacks of September 11, 2001, at the World Trade Center, the Pentagon, and Pennsylvania to realize the immeasurable emotional toll a traumatic event can have not only on the people directly affected by it, but also on others who witness it merely on television.

In 1995, the nation also suffered a most devastating trauma when innocent children, visitors and government workers were killed by a bomb that destroyed a federal building in Oklahoma City. The following year, a senior management official from the Division of Personnel at Health and Human Services, who visited the Oklahoma bombing site and interviewed federal government survivors there, reported that mangers were unable to deal with the aftermath of this tragedy. Supervisors were trying to go on as if nothing had happened—trying to go back to a "business as usual" mode, thereby failing to attend to the emotional needs of the employees who were recovering from this trauma. The result was disruption, loss of productivity, and decreased morale. Many of the employees who survived the explosion lost children who were in daycare in the building at the time.

Unfortunately, despite the highly qualified therapeutic care survivors may receive, many TLE employees are not given the attention they require on the job to readapt to their work environment. Some managers reveal considerable ambivalence in dealing with returning TLE employees. Some admit to having little or no idea how to make re-entry easier for them. Similarly, the TLE employee's co-workers are seldom able to understand the spectrum of emotional toll experienced by TLE employees and are also unsure how to behave toward them.

In my own research, I found that managers are seemingly in a quandary when dealing with a returning TLE employee. A number of questions confront them: What are the correct words of comfort to address to returning traumatized employees? How do I know if the traumatized person understands that he or she must go through a process of grief following the trauma? How do I help the employee deal with self-esteem issues? How do I deal with co-workers who may resent the traumatized employee's need for additional attention? What should I do when a traumatized employee does not want to do his or her work?

Most managers feel quite impotent in these situations. Their management training has not prepared them for the extraordinary demands of returning TLE employees and the extra burdens they may place on a manager's time, energy and patience. This imposition may develop into resentment by the manager and co-workers, if the manager is not able properly to deal with this management dilemma.

As reported by N. R. Kleinfield in an article in *The New York Times* (1996), some companies have recently begun to change their attitude toward employees. Employees who once considered the company their "family" have lost that sense of belonging. For example, Kleinfield reported that Chase Manhattan no longer wants to be a "parent" to its employees, it wants to be their "best friend." Companies are replacing their paternalistic attitude by trying to assist employees in becoming responsible for themselves. By offering courses and career counseling such companies hope to help them sharpen their skills and employability.

Survivors from a major layoff at Chase Manhattan, when it was taken over by Chemical Bank, were bitter because they had looked to management to take care of them until they retired. They had to face the fact that this was not going to happen. Those fired were traumatized by the event, and so were those who weren't. Chase Manhattan employees, who survived the cutoff, looking at all the empty desks surrounding them, still faced each day with trepidation and still wondered about their future. They were experiencing their own form of trauma, their jobs and livelihood hanging by a thread. People who are left stranded in situations like this must figure out how to cope on their own. How do managers handle such anxious people, when those managers themselves may be hanging by the same thread?

THE CHALLENGE AHEAD

Few researchers have explored the returning TLE employee experience. And no one, to my knowledge, has studied the powerful role that managers and co-workers can play in supporting the full emotional recovery of a TLE returning to the workplace.

According to Judith Lewis Herman (1992) in her book *Trauma and Recovery,* the essence of what a TLE employee feels coming back to work, is *disempowerment* and *disconnection.* TLE survivors feel incapable and incompetent to return to their former productive life. They feel disconnected from individuals such as co-workers and from the larger community of the workplace.

Helen Perlman (1993) in *Relationships: The Heart of Helping People* emphasizes that the healing necessary in situations following traumatic events occurs through empathic relationships. Thus, TLE survivors must renew connections with their managers and co-workers as well as with the broader work world. This is the only way they can re-establish the interpersonal elements that were damaged or destroyed by the traumatic experience.

Dr. Herman offers a process of recovery that unfolds in stages. Naming stages always helps to bring some clarity and order to a process that is painful, complex and inherently turbulent. While such stages are being "worked through" with a therapist, there are ways that managers and co-workers can support the emotional recovery process.

Understanding the emotional recovery process is central to the structure of this book and forms the basis for the contributions to recovery that managers and co-workers can provide to the returning TLE employee.

While many authors have written books describing the contributions psychiatrists and therapists may make in a TLE person's process through the stages of recovery, I have focused on the contributions the TLE person's managers and co-workers can make in understanding the emotional recovery process. It helps significantly when those fellow employees understand the dynamics of those recovery stages. I have summarized descriptions of this process from trauma into three stages. I have used a simple concept easily understood by the psychological layman to describe each stage.

The first of these three stages involves *putting out a welcome mat* for the returning trauma survivor, so TLE individuals may slowly gain control over their own physical reactions as well as emotional ones. They gradually begin feel welcome at work and to learn again to manage their environment effectively. A welcome mat is a symbol of a place that is safe and secure. In a workplace such feelings of safety and protection can only be developed through a personal support system. Though the professional therapist certainly provides a context of emotional security and protection for the survivor, the person's family, friends and co-workers help fill out the team that ultimately must produce this essential support system.

For example, when Diane called her boss to tell him of her daughter's automobile accident and surgery, if he had participated in a Study Circle on trauma and understanding emotional recovery, he would have known that the first thing Diane needed was to feel safe and secure about her work and her responsibilities. He could have *put out a welcome mat* for her by telling her to take as long as she needed to be with her daughter and not to worry about her responsibilities at the office. This would have given her some of the physical and emotional support she needed. Instead, his unsupportive response only created more anxiety and confusion for her. She was stunned by his apparent insensitivity to her situation. He also could have assured her that she would be paid for any time off she needed to take. While she was away, he could also have worked closely with her assistant to prepare for a smooth transition upon her return. Her assistant could have suggested to the staff that they welcome Diane back with a small breakfast meeting, giving her an opportunity to feel again the comfort of the work family—*a welcome mat.*

The second stage I like to call is *lending a listening ear.* For the survivor, being able to share her experience helps the survivor integrate both the trauma memory and the circumstances that led to the trauma. As survivors review their story with important people in their lives, they learn to deal with the traumatic event in a more realistic way. Among a returning TLE employee's "important people" are the individual's manager and certain co-workers.

For example, if her boss could have educated and enlisted the support of Diane's staff, it would have been very beneficial. Her boss could have alerted her employees about what had happened to Diane's daughter and encouraged them to approach her when she returned and *to lend a listening ear* if and as she chose to tell her trauma experience. Coming back to work after being out of the office for some time creates uncertainty and ambivalence for some traumatized people, because they really do not know what to expect when they open the office door on the first day back. Still under the influence of the traumatic experience, they may feel unsure how to behave or what to say to other people. Diane may want to talk about her trauma to people at work, or she may not. However, welcoming her back, acknowledging her situation and providing a listening ear would be helpful and supportive to her.

My third stage is called *offering a helping hand.* Its primary purpose is to initiate and re-establish the personal connections between the survivor and his or her community. During this stage, the TLE survivor must deal with creating a future and the development of a new self as well as new or restored relationships. Emerging from the traumatic environment of uncertainty, survivors may not know how to reach out to managers and co-workers to reclaim their place in the workplace world. It is up to the managers and co-workers to *offer a helping hand*, to respond positively and proactively to help restore these relationships. My purpose in writing this book is to show them how to do this appropriately.

This third, *offer a helping hand* stage, which involves re-linking the person to the work community, is very important since survivors of trauma like Diane will usually be distracted for the first few days or weeks back on the job. Her boss needs to know when and how to engage her about certain deadlines and gradually increase her workload, since its not unusual that trauma survivors like Diane may tire easily, feel confused and want to escape. For example, she may feel the need to go for a walk each day or want to begin an exercise program. Certainly, she will want to check in on her daughter during the day. It's important that-whatever she wants-as long as it is within reason- management give her all the *helping-hand* support she needs during this transitioning back and reconnecting to her work activity.

Returning TLE employees exist in all organizations, but most organizations do not have a method for supporting the three stages of emotional recovery that confront the returning TLE survivor.

It was apparent to me that what was lacking here was a short-term, essentially cost-free educational experience that could be conducted on-site especially for managers who supervise the re-entry of such employees, but also for the co-workers of TLE individuals since the co-workers are normally the ones who spend the most time with the survivor. Currently, in most organizations, professional counseling and therapy are usually made available to returning TLE employees. However, there seems to be no complementary, non-therapeutic intervention designed to teach managers and employees about the three stages of emotional recovery from trauma and how to create in the workplace an appropriate ambience for re-entry of TLE employees.

The Study Circle is an adult learning format that can do this. It's different from a focus group where there is only dialogue—a Study Circle requires action. It provides a structure so that managers and co-workers can explore a very sensitive personal and organizational challenge in an atmosphere of mutual respect and dialogue. Few other educational processes currently available in the business world can make this claim. The Study Circle can bring managers and employees together, as equals, to examine and discuss these emotional issues and find ways to apply in the workplace what they learn in the Study Circle.

When survivors like Diane return to a workplace that provides a *welcome mat* for them, a willing *listening ear* to listen to their trauma experience, and a *helping hand* to re-establish connections to the workplace family, they are more likely to recover more quickly and become once again fully productive members of the workplace team.

The rest of Part I of this book focuses on understanding the traumatic life experience (TLE) itself. Part II describes the Study Circle educational process, specifically the sessions on understanding the emotional recovery from trauma designed for managers and co-workers. Part III focuses on some special circumstances, for example, when trauma affects employees' children, when a traumatic event such as a bank robbery simultaneously affects a number of employees, and how traumatized persons can use personal and community resources to help themselves.

NOTE

1. *Healing the Wounds: Overcoming the trauma of layoffs and revitalizing down-sized organizations* (San Francisco: Jossey-Bass Publishers, (1993), p.39.

Chapter Two

What Is a Traumatic Life Experience (TLE)?

Technically, *a traumatic life experience (TLE) is a single unexpected, emotionally and physically overwhelming and utterly unwelcome event.* There are many, many TLEs. Some TLEs are sensational such as rapes, murders, suicides, burning buildings, natural disasters, kidnappings, explosions, terrorist attacks and hostage situations.

But other TLEs, the ones that don't make the headlines, can be just as devastating personally. Some of these include being diagnosed with a terminal illness, a job or career loss, losing a baby or having your teenager arrested for drunk driving. Although traumas like this are commonplace and happen to people every day, it doesn't mean they are any less emotionally crippling. We hear TLEs described frequently in more ordinary language. For example:

"When my wife told me she wanted a divorce, it knocked the wind out of my sails."

"When I got fired from my job, it dealt a major blow to my self-esteem and my career."

"When my home was burglarized, it completely wiped out my sense of security. No place was safe for me anymore."

"When my child was diagnosed with leukemia, it felt like getting punched in the face by a heavyweight boxing champion."

"When the policeman told me my son had been killed in an auto accident, my world came crashing down."

"When I had my heart attack, my entire future felt threatened."

"When my husband died so suddenly, it seemed like the end of everything."

"It may not seem important or tragic to you, but I have lived alone without family for most of my life, and when my Irish Setter Ruffy died, I lost my closest friend and companion for 17 years."

"When my son was arrested for dealing drugs, it made me feel like my whole life as a parent was a failure."

"I came into my neighborhood convenience store early one morning and found the owner, old Mr. Saul, dead on the floor. I find I can't go in that store any more. All I see is him dead on the floor."

"After I was raped, I felt utterly dirty and shameful, afraid to look anybody in the face."

"When the court awarded custody of my children to my spouse, I felt utterly powerless and helpless."

"When I was betrayed by my closest friend, my spirit was crushed. He literally took all the money I had and ran away."

"When the doctor told me my baby was Down syndrome, my life was turned upside down."

"When my husband ran off with another woman, I was shocked and enraged. How could I have been so naïve?"

"When my husband told me we had so many debts we had to declare bankruptcy, I had terrifying nightmares about dying old and poor."

WHERE AND WHEN TLES HAPPEN

Some TLEs happen directly to you, like a sudden life-changing illness, a holdup or a betrayal of trust. Some TLEs happen to those dear to you, your spouse, your children, your parents, your closest friends. Even though many traumatic experiences happen outside the workplace, they still have their effect on the workplace. This effect is seen in day's lost, substandard quality of work and the inability to perform with accustomed efficiency and effectiveness.

Some traumatic events happen at work, of course. The most newsworthy ones include an armed attack by a deranged gunman or an explosion perpetrated by a terrorist. Other group-experienced traumas include robberies, for example, where someone has broken into the building and stolen office computers; accidental fires that destroy the workplace and create panic among those locked inside; large scale layoffs through mergers; buyouts and bankruptcies of companies that leave people without jobs.

Understanding the emotional recovery process is often prolonged when many of the individuals in a workplace community have been traumatized by the same event. In another instance, the NASA team after the Challenger disaster, the employees of the federal building in Oklahoma City after the bombing, or the many thousands affected by the terrorist attack on the World Trade Center. Although mutual care and compassion can certainly help the healing process, usually some group therapy or group ritual is required to turn the tide toward recovery in the workplace when a group of employees have been traumatized by the same event.

Although recovery from traumatic events experienced by a whole group of employees is outside the scope of this book, I have included an appendix at the end of the book on this topic: "When a Group is Traumatized, How Do Managers and Employees Cope?"

WHAT ARE *NOT* TLES

There are many kinds of *chronic* traumas that fall also outside the scope of this book because they are far beyond the abilities of any manager or supervisor to deal with. They require serious and often prolonged medical and psychological help.

Those traumatized by chronic situations include, for example, servicemen day after day facing the violence and bloodshed of military combat and warfare. Children and spouses who have been continually sexually and physically abused over a period of years are wrenched with thoughts of anxiousness. People who have undergone severe physical and emotional deprivation in detention camps or hard-labor prisons, or even in prolonged homelessness living on the streets, also often have thoughts of negativity. People with severe mental and physical handicaps such as personality disorders or quadriplegia that can never be overcome. All of these are major traumatic situations, but they are not what I am calling a traumatic life experience.

In more ordinary, chronically stressful circumstances, certain people today are forced to live and work in continually trauma-producing situations: hospital nurses who work in intensive care units where more patients die than survive; wheelchair bound individuals continually challenged and frustrated by their handicaps; parents living with a drug or alcohol-addicted family member; a spouse living with a partner subject to bouts of depression, epilepsy or schizophrenia; mothers caring for a colicky baby for months on end; a single adult child having to care for a dying parent at home, especially one who is critical and complaining, family members living together in quarters that are too crowded; individuals living with a chronic debilitating illness such as asthma, lung cancer, or immune deficiency; diabetics living within a severely restricted diet. All of these are also major long-lasting traumatic situations, but they are not what I am calling a TLE.

The effects of such trauma-generating situations chronically and continually limit an employee's ability to perform naturally and normally. Usually, none of these employees afflicted by chronic traumatic situation can be helped by the approach suggested in this book. People like these are under such permanent or unremitting stress that the process of "recovery" that I present here has little application—though a managerial approach of compassion and care is never harmful. In chronic trauma, the situation is more or less permanent, or at least predictably recurring.

In contrast, the traumas focused on in this book are *single-event* traumatic experiences, not chronic or long-standing ones. A TLE is precisely *one* traumatic life experience, not a series of them or a persisting pattern of them. What I am calling *a Traumatic Life Experience (TLE) is a major single event whose traumatic effects temporarily limit the person's ability to act, respond and perform naturally and normally.*

AN INDIRECT TLE

As I mentioned, a person may be traumatized who was not the direct victim of the traumatic event. One manager in a large corporation told me that in one year, he had over a dozen traumatized parents who were affected not by something that had happened directly to them but by what had happened to their children. Here, in his own words, is how he described some of the traumas that affected his workplace:

1. "One of my fellow managers had a sixteen-year-old daughter who became pregnant by her same-age boyfriend; she was a brilliant high school student and her parents and teachers had planned a great college career for her. She got married instead. Her father is still not back to normal. "
2. Another mother was devastated when her son was arrested for armed robbery; she thinks it was all her fault for not bringing him up right.
3. One of our secretaries had a daughter arrested for using and selling drugs; she had absolutely no idea what was going on, and she still walks around feeling guilty, shameful and embarrassed.
4. One man's son, a victim in an auto accident, was hospitalized for spinal cord injuries; it about killed him when the doctors said his son would never walk again—and the kid was a great baseball player.
5. One of the nicest guys on our staff had a son who committed suicide; he's never been the same since and he keeps blaming himself.
6. Another great guy had a daughter who had a nervous breakdown; she's going to lose at least one year of school in a mental hospital. The father might just as well be there himself; he can only do a fraction of the work he used to do for us.

I've had parents who kids were held up at gunpoint, whose apartments were broken into and robbed, who had children born with major birth defects or born dead. Parents of these kids walk around the shop with their heads hung down for weeks and months.

Recently, I met with one of our managers, a father whose daughter had been raped. She was traumatized, but so was he. He went through periods of helplessness and rage—and it showed in his attitude at work. He felt inadequate as a parent because he was unable to protect her from the experience. The saddest example was one of our best technicians, a mother who was visiting her son in the hospital after a routine operation. By some error, the boy was given the wrong medication, he had an instant reaction to it, and he died within moments right in front of his mother. She has been under psychiatric care for months now.

In the past year, I have a number of employees who were also traumatized when something traumatic happened related to their spouse. One employee's spouse had a heart attack, another's committed suicide, another's was arrested for fraud and extortion, another's lost all the family savings gambling in Las Vegas, another's wrecked the car and killed someone while driving drunk, another's was diagnosed with pancreatic cancer and given only a few months to live, another's ran off abandoning her and taking all their money, another's ran off with their two young children.

These are just a sample of the single events that shock and traumatize people and change their lives, their self-image, their self-confidence, and their self-worth.

The point is that traumatic life experiences are all around us. Not even counting those produced by violence in the workplace—shootings, hostage situations, suicides, arson, physical or sexual assault, acts of sabotage against equipment or property—there are countless other cases of traumatic life experiences. They have many physical and emotional consequences that employees bring with them as they return to work, trying to recover from their trauma.

These are the kinds of survivors that managers and co-workers can help in the workplace.

Chapter Three

What Is It Like to Be
a Returning TLE Employee?

Edward, a 55-year-old bachelor, had been an employee of the United States Postal Service for 34 years. During all these years he had lived with his mother, who recently died at 79 of a heart attack. His manager, knowing how close Edward was to his mother, told him to take a full week off. When Edward returned to his post office job, he found himself unable to get into his familiar efficient routine, even though he told his manager it felt good to be back among his fellow employees and it felt miserable being alone at home. However, during the day, amid all the hustle and bustle around him, Edward would sit at his desk and stare into space for long periods of time. One co-worker heard him sobbing in the men's room. To fellow employees it seemed he always kept wanting to talk about his mother and to repeat stories about her that they had all heard before.

Ellemeta, a robust, strong-willed, middle-aged divorced woman who lived alone, worked in the same postal office as Edward. Her trauma was being robbed in her home by a masked and armed intruder. He had come in through a window while she was asleep. As he held her at gunpoint, she went into shock shaking in silence in her bed. He said he wanted only cash and jewelry. She obediently told him where he could find what he wanted. He had come and gone in less than five minutes, but those few minutes were burned into her memory. "My home was violated," she explained to a friend later on. "It was like being raped. To think I was *that* vulnerable!" Although Ellemeta reported the robbery to the police, there was little hope of catching the thief as he had been wearing a mask and gloves. They told her she was a "lucky" one and to think about putting iron bars on her windows. When she came back to work a few days later, she wasn't at all quiet and subdued like Edward. She ranted and raved. She was outraged and frustrated. She cursed the intruder with all the vituperatives she could think of. She told co-workers what she should have done and would do if it happened again. She wouldn't be caught helpless and vulnerable the next time. She would get a gun, or she would move.

There is no such thing as a standard TLE employee returning to the workplace, because no two people will react to a traumatic event in exactly the same way. Some, like Edward, will come back to work quiet, tentative and hesitant. Others, like Ellemeta, will return angry, bitter or even enraged. Still others will walk into the office feeling confused, frightened and even ashamed.

TRAUMATIC LIMITATIONS

What we do know is that, when a traumatized person returns to work, the effects of the traumatic event generally *limit the person's ability to act, respond, perform and make decisions naturally and normally.* Because of this, such survivors of trauma, when they first return to the workplace, usually need a social readjustment period. This readjustment period will certainly last much longer than one day, and can sometimes stretch out into weeks, depending on the employee's personality and the severity and shock of the traumatic event.

Psychologists tell us that individuals who have never been traumatized before generally have an easier time in recovery. They are not as likely to be as devastated as those who have experienced multiple traumas in their lifetime, especially childhood traumas. In this sense, our emotional systems are like our muscular systems. If you have strained your back a number of times before now, you are more likely to strain it again when you try lifting something heavy than someone who has never had a strained back.

Wherever we have been emotionally wounded before in a certain area we are more vulnerable there than in other areas where we have not been wounded. For example, two people can be in the same auto accident; one may be severely traumatized by the event with its effects lasting for months or years, while the other person seems to bounce back to normal very quickly and is able to drive again without fear. Psychology says that the odds are that the first person had been traumatized similarly before this, and that the second person had never been in a similar traumatic situation.

PERSONALITY TYPES RESPOND DIFFERENTLY

Of course, after a traumatic life experience, different personality types will react differently and process the event differently. Introverts, typically, like

Edward, when they return to work after a TLE may not want to talk about the event. If you confront them about it, they often resist revealing their inner feelings and will tend to stay focused on surface behavior, activities and tasks. Like Edward, they may go to the rest room and cry alone.

In contrast, an extraverted returning TLE employee, like Ellemeta, will need to talk about the experience and express feelings, unless those feelings are shameful or embarrassing, which they usually prefer to hide or camouflage.

Extraverts will sometimes tend to go to emotional extremes when they return to work; they might appear either over-confident or utterly despondent. Consequently, in the period after their return they might require frequent renegotiation of workplace tasks and deadlines. Ellemeta, who usually waited on postal customers up front, was in no shape to deal with outside customers her first few days back, and she knew it, so her manager assigned her to work in the sorting room for the time being, where she could vent her emotions without upsetting customers.

TRAUMA AND GRIEF

Almost every traumatic life experience (TLE) is also a traumatic *loss* experience. As such, part of the TLE's emotional recovery from trauma involves some amount of grief work. Wherever there is loss, there will be grief. While Edward's trauma involved losing a beloved human being, Ellemeta's trauma involved losing her sense of security. Others lose their jobs, their spouses, their children, and their money. Those who have been betrayed, lose their sense of trust in humanity. Some lose their self-respect. Others lose hope. In all these cases, they must learn to work through their grief. It is part of the trauma recovery process.

G. Engel (1961) in an article in *Psychosomatic Medicine* was the first person to compare emotional *loss* with a physical wound. In both cases the wound must heal, which takes time. As a wound heals, first a scab is formed; it is the body's way of protecting the wound as it heals. When the scab falls off by itself, it is nature telling us that the healing is complete. In a similar way, a trauma is an emotional wound and, in the healing process the mind forms an emotional protective scab. But, nature alone will not bring about the necessary healing; it requires the loving care of other human beings before the "scab" eventually falls away.

Engel (1961) sees grief and trauma work as a healthy process that slowly heals the wounds of the psyche. His article is entitled "Is Grief a Disease?" *Psychosomatic Medicine.* Grief is not a disease but, he cautions, it can develop into one. "It is possible to die of a "broken heart.""[1]

EVEN PSYCHOLOGISTS CAN BE TRAUMATIZED

Dr. John Schneider, (1984) a noted clinical psychologist, in his book, *Stress, Loss and Grief*, tells about his own job counseling clients who are terminally ill and depressed. During a single week in his practice, three of his clients died, another attempted suicide and was hospitalized. During the same week he witnessed a young woman killed by a train near his office. After these incidents, he found himself unable to be effective with his clients because of his own grief. Shortly after this, another client committed suicide. This led him to question the usefulness of his own work. Reflecting on his own experience, he suggested that trauma could produce intense fear, helplessness, loss of control and loss of memory, as merely witnessing trauma and hearing about the traumas of others had done for him during that week. He noticed that his usual problem-solving abilities began to malfunction. Though he could carry out routine activities, like dress himself, answer the phone or ride the subway, he was not able to respond well to new circumstances.

More generally, he found that most trauma survivors were a lot like him. They tend to change their behavior. They become fixated on well-controlled tasks, things they know they can do well without thinking. They also tend to isolate themselves. Their reality and perceptions are blurred. Sometimes they hallucinate; they see and react to things that are not there. They are grieving.

In his book *The Art of Condolence*, Leonard M. Zunin (1991), a psychiatric consultant and authority on attachment and loss, notes that bereavement trauma is associated with changes in behavior that encompass relationships with others in their day-to-day activities. For grieving persons, the simplest activities, such as paying the bills or doing housekeeping chores, may feel like major burdens. He points out that traumatized persons commonly feel as though they are falling apart.

David S. Sobel, M.D. (1994) in an article titled "RX: Surviving Traumatic Experience" maintains that survivors of a traumatic experience lose their sense of control and their connection to others. For some, their life meaning is brought into question when they are dealing with the aftermath of a trauma. At the moment of trauma, most victims are rendered powerless; trust in others is lost and they feel abandoned.

PHYSICAL SYMPTOMS

In my own research, I found that physical health symptoms are generally the most obvious signs displayed by the returning TLE employee. They include nausea, insomnia, headaches, lack of appetite, increased alcohol consumption and fatigue. These symptoms are also likely to be the most disruptive in the workplace. Sometimes, when physical health problems resulting from the trauma manifest themselves after an employee has returned to work, the employee must take time off. These problems will certainly affect the organization's level of productivity.

The effects of traumatic life experiences may be more pronounced in a person with poor mental or physical health. In her book *Necessary Losses*, Judith Viorst (1986) claims those with a poor history of mental or physical health are at greater risk. She states that loss through death is a major life stressor and if a person endures additional stressors in his life at the time, the risk of mental health and vulnerability to illness increases.

There are eight million Americans every year who experience death in their immediate family. There are 800,000 new widowers and widows annually, and 400,000 children die every year before they reach the age of twenty-five. According to the Institute of Medicine of the National Academics, "those who experience loss without the support of a social network tend to find the trauma more intense."

SURVIVORS OF JOB LOSS

Loss can happen in many different ways. For example, when employees of a major telephone company lost their jobs because of re-organization, the employees who remained went through an identity crisis. Author and organizational consultant William Bridges (1988) in his book *Surviving Corporate Transition* reveals this identity crisis.

When an organization is going through significant change, confused and empty feelings can pervade the corridors and offices. . . People go about their tasks mechanically, and an outsider might think that things are going smoothly. But they are not. People's minds and hearts are elsewhere. In spite of the fact that there is more to do than ever, the employees move like people in a dream or waste their days in endless bickering. People talk but do not communicate; they listen but they do not hear. The days pass with little getting done.

Katherine S. Newman (1988), an anthropologist at Columbia University, studied unemployed managers who were once secure in their jobs. In her book, *Falling from Grace: the Experience of Downward Mobility in the American Middle Class*, she describes managers who were unable to cope after losing their jobs. They became depressed, embittered, stopped taking care of themselves, started drinking and lost contact with their families and friends. Some committed suicide. She asserts that people at the management level often inappropriately blame themselves for what happened. Such managers buy into the cultural belief that "a manager succeeds because of his own hard work"[2] (p. 38). Whenever successful managers fall from grace, that traditional ideology boomerangs. This produces a psychological trauma that Barry Glassner called a "career crash."[3] If individuals believe they are responsible for their own destinies, there is no one else to blame in case of a failure.

According to Glassner (1994) in his book *Career Crash: The New Crisis and Who Survives*, there are many routes to a career crash, the fastest and surest one is to be fired. In the 1990s, downsizing became a routine part of American life, and the most common path to career loss. Glassner's research includes a survey of 250 managers who had spent from six months to two years seeking a new job. The survey revealed that people in their mid-thirties to mid-fifties have the hardest time finding employment. Only 55 percent of those surveyed had succeeded, compared to 67 percent of managers who were either younger or older.

He also interviewed people who lost their jobs. These interviews revealed fear of looking for another position; the sheer shock of being out of work; embarrassment at having to tell their parents, children and spouses; and hurt and anger at the company to which they had committed their loyalty. An employee whom Glassner interviewed shared the following with him.

I'd never been involved in anything where I could be called a failure or less than extremely successful . . . I was raised to believe that if you keep your nose clean and do a good job, you'll be rewarded. On some level, of course, I knew that wasn't true anymore. In fact, I'd laid off people myself during an earlier cutback. But knowing about it and going through it yourself are two different things (p. 35).

Nothing brings home more the debilitating power of a traumatic life experience than having one yourself.

NOTES

1 *Healing Pain: Attachment, Loss and Grief Therapy.* (London and New York: Routledge, 1987), p. 13.

2. *Falling from Grace: The Experience of Downward Mobility in the American Middle Class.* (New York: Free Press, 1988), p. 38.

3. *Career Crash: The New Crisis and Who Survived.* (New York & London: Simon & Schuster, 1994), p. 35.

Chapter Four

What Can Managers Do?

THE FIRST DAY BACK TO WORK

If you are a manager, the odds are that in the last few months you probably had more than one employee who needed a number of days off because they had been through a traumatic life experience and were deeply emotionally affected by it.

What do you say to such people, like Edward and Ellemeta, when they first return to the workplace? What is the most appropriate way to treat such people when they come back? You realize you are not a professional counselor or therapist. You are not an employee assistance expert. You have not been trained in psychology, nor do you claim to understand the subtle workings of the human psyche or the stages of understanding emotional recovery from a traumatic life experience. You're a manager.

You would like to do some good for the returning employee and yet you do not want to cause any emotional harm.

There are many ways to be harmful, or at least to hinder the emotional recovery process, even with the best of intentions. TLE employees returning to the workplace for the first time have reported to me ways their managers and supervisors showed little or no sensitivity to the powerful emotional effects the TLE had on them.

Here are a few *don'ts* suggested by those TLE employees whose experience upon return to the workplace was unhelpful. These are their requests to managers and supervisors:

Don't avoid us. Don't remain silent or aloof when we return to work, as if the trauma had never happened and everything was back to normal.

"My manager may have been unsure of the best way to welcome me back as an employee or afraid he would say the wrong thing," explained one who

24

remembered his first day back on the job. "The worst thing he did was to avoid me as if I had some contagious disease. I took his silence and avoidance as a clear message that he didn't really care about me or what happened to me, and that I didn't deserve his attention."

Don't start off talking to us about company problems and your problems.

"This happened to me," explained a woman about her first day back to work after her husband's heart attack. "My manager, who happens to be a woman, started in about how bad things were for her. She started listing all the problems she had at the office. She never asked about how I was feeling or how ready for work I was. I guess she simply wanted me to forget my traumatic experience—as if I could!—and expected me to go back to my desk as usual, as if nothing emotionally upsetting had ever happened."

A much better approach might have been to tell the returning employee how important and valuable she was to the office staff and how much she was needed and appreciated. As it came out, the manager was communicating the message, "Look how bad my life is, too. You think you have problems? Just look at mine."

Don't lay big expectations on us at the start.

"My manager, the day I came back, told me that he had a big project waiting for me that he wanted me to take charge of," said one woman who had just returned from a miscarrying a baby. "He told me that keeping me busy would take my mind off my 'situation.'"

If a TLE employee could say one thing to a manager, it would be something like this: *"I need to feel safe and secure here in the workplace. I need to feel that you will protect me from harm."* Most returning employees couldn't formulate their needs that clearly, but it is what they most need and want.

They don't want to be coddled as a child, but they do want managers and their co-workers to respect them for the fact that they have survived a powerfully negative emotional experience and may need time t recover from its effects.

EIGHT STEPS FOR THE FIRST MEETING

Here are some first steps a manager should take as soon as a TLE employee returns to work, even before he or she sits down at a desk or starts to work

1. You, as manager, should initiate the first contact.

Do not wait for the employee to come to you. As soon as they arrive on their first day back to work, greet such employees with a quiet smile. Welcome them back. Tell them they have been missed. No need for backslapping or other overly enthusiastic greetings.

2. Carry out your first dialogue privately in a quiet place.

Do it preferably in your office with the door closed. Ask a secretary to hold all phone calls. This tells the returning employee that you want to create a safe place for him or her. Remember, during these first days, your main task is to help returning TLE employees find their own level of comfort and security. Some may need much more reassurance than others. Let yourself be totally present to the employee as you talk, not distracted by reading mail or marking reports on your desk.

3. Be as composed as you can.

Gently look the returning employee in the eye. Don't avoid eye contact, but don't force it either. Some employees feel shame and embarrassment about their traumatic experiences. When the employee looks back at you, he or she should see someone who is calm and compassionate. The returning employee does not need to feel strong emotions from you. Your presence should be supportive and responsive to their needs. Certainly, don't put pressure on the employee to get back to the job with phrases like, "Have we got a backlog of work waiting for you!" or "You sure have a lot of catching up to do!"

4. Be aware of the fears the returning employee may have.

No need to quiz the person on their fears. You can presume that fears are present. If at all possible, assure returning employees that their job is secure and waiting for them whenever they are ready to take it up again.

Some fears that returning TLE employees may have include:

Fear that I will lose, or have already lost my old job.

Fear that I am being, or have already been, replaced.

Fear that the person who covered for me while I was gone did a better job than I ever did.

Fear that, even if I have my job back, I won't be able to perform as well as I used to.

Fear that I won't be as fast or effective as I used to be.

Fear that I won't have the physical strength to handle my job—or catch up.

Fear that I will get emotionally upset and it will affect the quality of my work.

Fear that the pressures of the job will now overwhelm me.

Fear that I will make many mistakes because I get easily distracted these days.

Fear that I can't meet deadlines.

Fear that I will break down and cry during a meeting.

Fear that my co-workers will have negative thoughts about me, for example, that I am a bad spouse or parent.

Fear that my co-workers will pity me or feel sorry for me.

Fear that they will laugh at me behind my back.

Fear that my managers and co-workers will expect more than I can give right
now.
Fear that I may be seen as a weak person for needing time off.
Fear that they will avoid me.
Fear that they will try to pry into my personal life.

Of course, no returning employee will have all of these fears, but all TLE
employees will have some of them or others like them. The traumatic experience has undermined their basic feelings of safety and security. They return to
work feeling very vulnerable. Each of the fears listed above reflect that loss.

*5. Make certain that the employee is getting all possible professional help
that the company provides.*

Make sure the employee is familiar with the Employee Assistance Program
and is receiving therapy or counseling, if it is needed or wanted by the employee. Many employees are unaware of an organization's resources and how
to access them. Whenever possible, you should facilitate the process, perhaps
even walking with the employee to the EAP office or offering to help fill out
complicated forms.

Reassure returning employees that the company wants to help provide for
their health. Among some people, there is still a sense of stigma or shame in
seeing a psychologist or psychiatrist. Assure such employees that everyone
encounters emotionally overwhelming times, and most people need psychological help in working through such stress. Such help is desirable and necessary for a healthy emotional recovery.

For your information, there are a number of consequences of trauma that
may require professional help. Some of these signs in a returning TLE employee are:

Difficulty setting limits and boundaries with others.
A continuing sense of isolation.
Strong feelings of worthlessness and powerlessness.
Strong feelings of shame and guilt.
Severe damage to self-esteem and self-image.
Hypersensitivity and overreaction to normal situations.
Suicidal gestures or attempts.
Making threats of violence in the workplace.
Making threats of physical harm to others.
Depression or emotional deprivation.
Addiction or substance abuse.
Tendency to sabotage success.
Tendency to be victimized by others.

When you notice one or more of these symptoms in a returning TLE employee, especially if it persists beyond a few days, gently and compassionately check to see if the employee is under professional care. If not, see that appropriate care is found.

Neither you, as a manager, nor your other employees, are expected to deal with such symptoms and issues since they require professional help. Please do not attempt to play the role of psychotherapist with a returning employee. Nor, in cases of violence in the workplace, are you expected to replace the security team or law enforcement. Your role along with co-workers is simply to provide an emotionally safe environment for the trauma survivor, to let the person tell their story if they wish, and to re-establish personal connection with the individual.

6. Conduct the interview in a non-threatening way by asking only open-ended questions.

If you need to interact, ask very general questions like:

Do you need anything?
Is there anything I can help you with? Doctor appointments? Schedules?
How can I be helpful?
Are you getting enough support at home?
Do you have any questions about your re-entry?
Do you feel unsure or hesitant about anything?
Is there anything specifically that you want or need today?
How can I help you get what you need?
What types of work do you feel up to?
Do you feel comfortable going back to your regular desk?
Is there anything you'd like me to say to your co-workers? Any requests?
Is there anything you want to know from me?
Is there anything you want me to know?
Is there anything you want to talk to me about?

Trust that the returning employee knows what he or she needs. Don't presume that you know better than they what they need at the moment. That's why open-ended questions are the best. The way the employee answers your open-ended questions will direct your conversation and tell you how to proceed.

7. Establish a re-entry program with the employee's cooperation and input.

Find out from the returning TLE employee how much he or she feels ready to attempt during the first few days. Together, set up a re-entry plan suggesting how much and how soon assignments can get done. Invite the employee to report, perhaps each day for the first week or so, how the re-entry program is working. Clearly allow for such a program to be revised at the will of the employee. Don't presume you know what the employee can or cannot do at this time. In most cases, they themselves do not even know what they are capable of, especially if the trauma was shocking. Remember, the employee needs to feel secure in the workplace. If they are given more assignments than they can deal with, they will be emotionally overwhelmed and experience failure, which is not conducive to a safe and secure situation.

8. Promise you will initiate regular contact with the returning employee. And keep your promise.

Invite the employee to come to see you whenever he or she wishes to or feels a need to. If the employee does not initiate a visit within the next few days, you should suggest a meeting and find a quiet time and place for it. Ask some of the same open-ended questions listed above. They reinforce in the employee's mind that you intend to maintain a safe and secure environment for them. This is the best thing you can do to promote an understanding toward their emotional adjustment of their trauma.

In such future meetings, you may also ask about their worries, their difficulties readjusting, how adequately the company is caring for them, their own personal agendas, hopes and dreams. In this way, if they wish, they may choose to share with you their trauma experience and what happened to them in some detail. This is a good sign that the survivor feels comfortable with you.

A SUCCESSFUL RE-ENTRY

Here is a story told to me by one of the managers who had attended a Study Circle on the returning TLE employee.

Susan was one of the most outgoing and caring people in our office. She was only in her early thirties, so we were all shocked and worried when we heard that, after a routine physical, she was diagnosed with breast cancer requiring a radical mastectomy. Needless to say, it was traumatic for Susan herself, the diagnosis coming as a total surprise. An operation was scheduled within days. Susan called me, her manager, to let me know what had happened. Her usual cheerful voice was somber and strained with emotion. She didn't know exactly when she would be back to work. Maybe it would take a number of weeks.

She called again after the operation to say the doctors thought it was successful. "But you never know," she said.

I asked her if she would be willing to accept cards and phone calls from people in the office. She was agreeable to that, and said how she missed the people at work. "The doctors told me I'd be pretty tired after chemotherapy and radiation, but I guess I can talk on the phone." She said, a number of the women from the office phoned and chatted with her from time to time, keeping her connected with people and events in the office.

One day, I had a phone call from Susan. "The doctors say I can start back to work next week as long as I take it easy. They don't want me to exhaust myself. If it's okay with you, I'd love to come back, at least part time," She said, I noticed that she had that old sparkle in her voice again, so I assured her that she would be most welcome.

"I have a special favor to ask," she began. "You know that with chemotherapy, your hair falls out. I was no exception. Right now I'm bald as an eagle. People have been telling me I should wear a wig, but you know me. I've never tried to hide anything. I'll wear bright scarves and various things to cover my head, but underneath I'll be bald. Do you think the gang at the office can tolerate a bald Susan in their midst?"

"What made you decide to take this approach?" I asked with genuine interest.

"Well," she said, "I'm doing it to remind me that I am a cancer survivor. I don't want to upset anybody in the office, but I also don't want to hide the fact of what I've been going through. I've finally realized there's nothing to be ashamed of about having cancer," she said. I complimented her on her courage and said I thought the office staff could handle her brightly-covered head.

On the next day, I called the office staff together for a short meeting, told them that Susan would be coming back part-time, that she was a courageous woman, and that she decided against hiding the fact that she had lost all her hair from chemotherapy. I told them what she had told me about being proud to be a cancer survivor, and how she didn't like to hide anything from those she considered her friends. I told them that Susan's cancer was a traumatic life experience, and while the doctors were working to help Susan's heal her cancer, our job was to help her recover from the effects of her trauma. I reminded them that, to do this, we needed to create an emotional *welcome mat* for Susan in the office, and we should provide a *listening ear* to let her tell her story if she wished to, and that we should provide a *helping hand* to reconnect with her gently but lovingly.

I asked if anyone had any questions. Someone asked how we were supposed to make her feel safe. To my surprise, a number of people immediately volunteered suggestions about what they thought they could do. That triggered other ideas. In a short time, we felt we could provide a secure environment and we were all excited about welcoming Susan back.

On her first day back to work, Susan came directly to my office, as I had suggested to her over the phone the night before. She was wearing a bright red bandana over her head. We talked a bit about how she felt coming back. She said she felt a bit anxious that the office staff would think she was weird because she came to work with a bald head, that they would avoid her because she had cancer, and that she might find her self exhausted and tired out right in the middle of some meeting, which would embarrass her. I assured her that we were all ready for her. And we were.

After lunch, Susan came to my office, almost in tears, saying how great everyone had been to her and how all her fears about not being accepted had been groundless. "I even got compliments on my red bandana," she said.

Chapter Five

What Do You Tell Co-Workers?

HELPFUL CO-WORKERS

Even though you as a manager can have a strong influence on understanding the emotional recovery of a returning TLE employee, in the long run it is the employee's co-workers who are likely to have more continual and closer contact than you. Therefore, they can be very helpful in promoting the re-entry process for such employees. You and the co-workers can assist returning employees by how you respond to them.

Like you, the returning employee's co-workers may be unsure of the most appropriate way to treat the returning trauma survivor.

Like you, they can give unhelpful responses as well as helpful ones—provided they know the difference.

Like you, fellow employees, feeling less than competent and confident in dealing with trauma survivors, may want to avoid the returning employee and not mention the traumatic topic. In their hesitancy and anxiousness, they may prefer to act as though the traumatic experience had never happened and that everything is now perfectly normal—as if the employee had merely been absent for a few days with the flu. A lot of us are like that.

Avoidance and denial from co-workers are not helpful responses to the returning TLE employee.

Although it would be better if most or many of the co-workers had received some educational instruction in a Study Circle or workshop about the process of emotional recovery from trauma, you as their manager can give them a short course in the emotional recovery process plus a few simple but effective suggestions for treating a returning TLE employee.

A SHORT COURSE IN TRAUMA
AND EMOTIONAL RECOVERY

As manager, you might say something to co-workers like the following:

There are three steps in understanding the emotional recovery from trauma. We all need to know them because Sarah will be coming back to work tomorrow after her husband's death [insert the appropriate name and traumatic event] and we want to do all we can to assist in her recovery and re-entry here. We can be very helpful.

1. Provide a Welcome Mat

The first stage in understanding the emotional recovery is that the TLE employee (Sarah, in this case) needs to feel save and secure here at work. It is our job to create a welcoming place for her. Such people, like Sarah, returning to work, depending on the nature of their traumatic experience, may have different emotions. Sarah, having experienced the sudden loss of a loved one, might feel helpless or grieving. We might notice that during the day she is unusually quiet or lost in her thoughts. Another person returning to work who had been robbed on the street may feel suspicious and afraid. We might notice that such a person is jumpy and easily startled. A woman returning to us who had been raped may feel shameful, so she may want to avoid talking to us. A mother whose child was arrested for drugs may feel guilty. She may want to avoid talking to you as well. A person who is returning after a stroke or heart attack may feel tired or weak. They may seem forgetful or unable to find their way around.

So, any kind of teasing, name-calling, demands or criticisms are out of place. They make the survivor feel unsafe and insecure. On the opposite side, if you avoid the person or act as though they hadn't experienced a traumatic event, they will not feel safe either, for by your silence you are, in effect, denying their reality. What is real is that they had a traumatic experience, and you need in some way to acknowledge that fact. Acknowledgment doesn't take very much effort. It is enough to say, "I'm sorry for your loss." Or "I heard what happened. That was terrible. I'm sorry."

2. Provide a Listening Ear

The second stage of understanding the emotional recovery involves assisting them if they choose to retell and reconstruct their trauma experience. Much of the necessary work at this stage will happen between the survivor and a counselor or therapist. It is professional work. But all of us can still be helpful here. For example, if the returning employee wants to tell you the story of what happened, let them tell you. But let them tell it to you in their own way, at their own speed, and in their own time. Don't probe. Don't try to force them to tell you the story and don't outright ask them to tell you all about it. That would make the situation emotionally unsafe for them. And we never want to make it unsafe. Rather, make a simple offer, especially if you are a good friend, and say, "If you ever need to talk about what happened, I'll be glad to listen." And leave it at that.

It is not ever helpful to a returning TLE employee—on the first day back or a week later—to confront the person by saying, "Tell me all about it. I want to hear everything." This might seem more like a demand than an invitation. Such a demand would be an invasion of the person's inner feelings and immediately creates an unsafe place, for it is forcing the employee to talk about something that may be very personal and private. Honoring the person's privacy is a way of keeping her safe and protected.

3. Lend a Helping Hand

The third stage in understanding the emotional traumatized person is their need to belong to the community they left. And we can help in that process. The traumatic life experience has in many ways severed the survivor's connection with her family, neighbors and her workplace colleagues. We may not think that anything has changed, but the TLE employee does. The traumatic experience has changed Sarah; she does not see herself as the same person she was before the event. A short time ago, she saw herself as a married woman looking forward to a future with her husband. Now she must learn to see herself as a widow facing the future alone. Her very identity has been affected.

Whether the traumatic event was a rape, a heart attack or, as in Sarah's case, the sudden loss of an immediate family member, it has changed the survivor's self-image. So, just as Sarah must find ways as a widow to reconnect to her family and neighbors, she also needs to get reconnected here at work in her new social status. And we can all help her do that. Not only does Sarah need us to create a safe place for her, she needs us to help her reconnect to us and to her job. Sarah may physically look the same to you when she returns, but inside she will probably feel different from the woman who left here a week ago. So, in some ways you may need to treat her as a "new" employee. Very gently. You may need to coach or help her a bit on her job. In other words, lend a helping hand. Don't expect her immediately to jump right back into her old groove. Don't be surprised if, for a time, she is a bit slower, a bit less effective and efficient than she used to be. She is dealing with much emotional distress and grief. Just reconnect with her gently.

SUMMARY

To sum up, the three stages in the recovery process are:

1. Put out a welcome mat: Create a safe and secure workplace atmosphere for the returning TLE employee.
2. Lend a listening ear. Let the survivor tell their story or trauma experience to you, but only if they need to and want to.
3. Offer a helping hand: Help them get reconnected to you, to the other co-workers and to their jobs.

SOME SUGGESTIONS

Here are some quick suggestions to give to co-workers of the returning TLE employee. Tell them you too are following these suggestions, since they are the same for everyone.

1. Welcome the returning TLE employee warmly and compassionately.
    Make them feel safe here. Acknowledge their traumatic experience simply and very generally with something, such as, "Welcome back, George. I was sorry to hear about your son's auto accident." Or, "Good to have you back, Helen. I heard what happened. I'm sorry." Or, "Mary, I'm sorry about what happened, but I'm glad to see you. Is there any way I can be helpful? If you have any questions, I'll be at my desk."
2. Remember that, even though trauma survivors may look fine on the outside, they are going through a lot of inner turmoil.
    Many of them feel confused or may have trouble concentrating. They may be easily frustrated or discouraged. They may have trouble staying focused on their work or seem to lack the energy for it. Some may feel anxiety and fear, others shame or guilt, still others anger and frustration. They may not be sleeping well at night. They may feel nauseous. They may have lost their appetite. They may be bothered by headaches. They may start drinking. They are probably re-experiencing their traumatic event over and over in their imagination during the day. In themselves, these scary memories may lead to many distractions and a lack of the ability to concentrate. But the person can no more choose to stop the images of their trauma from resurfacing than you could choose to stop yourself from a sudden sneeze. Just be patient with them. Your job is always to create and maintain a safe environment for them.

3. Find simple ways to re-establish connections to you and to the workplace.

Invite them to join you for lunch or at one of the break times. Team up with them on their projects or yours. Affirm each time they initiate or cooperate with an act of reconnection. "I noticed you and Phil working together this morning. He missed you and is really glad you're back." Or, "I noticed you were talking to Sally in the break room. I'm glad she's a friend of yours. She was worried about you while you were away."

RECONNECTING BEFORE RETURNING TO WORK

Tom had been rushed to the hospital after a heart attack he suffered lifting his daughter's heavy suitcases into the trunk of her car. It was after Thanksgiving dinner, and he was getting her ready for the drive back to college. He collapsed on the driveway. Soon the ambulance came. After a week in the hospital, he recuperated at home for another four weeks before his doctor allowed him to go back to work—but only on a part-time basis.

Tom's manager at work had been notified of the heart attack and hospitalization the day after it happened. But he decided that he and Tom's co-workers should not get involved and should leave Tom alone during this time, to be with his wife and family. The manager thought he was doing the best thing for Tom, presuming Tom would be embarrassed for co-workers to see him in his weakened state. His assumption was very mistaken.

When Tom finally came back to work, he looked sad. He confided to one of his co-workers, "I never had a single card or phone call or visit from any of the guys and gals here at the shop. I really felt abandoned by everybody."

The manager could have helped Tom's adjustment of re-entry very easily by contacting his wife and asking if Tom would like cards, phone calls or visitors. If Tom or his wife had said that Tom *didn't* want any contact from the workplace that would have been a clear message. On the contrary, if Tom had wished to keep connected to his friends at work, they could have been fostering his recovery for all these weeks. They would have been supporting him by keeping him reconnected to the workplace community.

Even if Tom's response had been to refuse contact with co-workers—he may have felt too weak to cope with them at that moment—the manager could have suggested that he or another employee be contacted if Tom changed his mind. Also, the manager could still call Tom's wife from time to time to let Tom know, through her, that he was thought of and cared about at the workplace.

Whenever a recuperating TLE employee at home welcomes contact from co-workers, it is a healthy sign. A manager can pass on to fellow employees the survivor's wish for contact. In this way, forms of connection are not only welcome but also become a healing force. For such an employee who remains connected to co-workers while hospitalized or at home, workplace re-entry will be easier and more satisfying. But such contact should always be at the discretion of the TLE employee.

TYPICAL QUESTIONS CO-WORKERS MAY ASK YOU

We live in an age where information on any subject is available on television, in books or on line. For all that availability, people remain relatively uninformed especially about psychological matters. But, when they are confronted with a situation where they need information, most people are curious and will ask questions. As a manager, you will want to know how to answer some of their questions about trauma and emotional recovery. Here are a few of the most common.

What Does The Employee Coming Back to Work for the First Time Feel Like?

Most traumas involve an important loss. Some returning TLE employees may have lost a spouse, a child, a parent, a home, a job, a career, their physical security, their financial security, their social standing, their reputation, their honor, or their hopes. As a result, the returning employees perceive *themselves* differently, even though they may look the same to you.

One woman may have been a happy and proud mother before her trauma, but returns to work as a childless mother or the mother of a criminal. Her "self" has a new—and unwelcome—meaning. Her inner identity, the way she sees herself, has changed.

A man may have been climbing the ladder of success in his company before his heart attack, but he returns to work realizing that the kinds of career promotions he had been looking forward to will probably not happen to him. His ladder has no more rungs on it.

How Does the Returning Employee Perceive Managers and Co-Workers?

There is no single answer to this question. It depends on a combination of factors including the nature and seriousness of the trauma as well as the personality of the returning TLE employee and his relationships with manager and co-workers.

For example, if the person has been raped or their child has been arrested as a drug dealer, the returning employee may feel ashamed, defensive, guilty or embarrassed, and not want to face co-workers. They think other employees may look at them as at fault, weak, ineffective, unworthy or a failure, and they fear the others will not want to associate with them or are saying negative things about them.

Other traumatic experiences, like being robbed or having one's car rammed into by a careless driver without insurance, may generate anger and frustration. Such returning employees may expect co-workers to be sympathetic and share their irate feelings.

The returning TLE employee's personality makes a difference, too. With those who tend to hide their feelings, you may never know how they perceive themselves or what their needs are. Others who wear their hearts on their sleeves will usually tell you how they feel about themselves and indicate how they would like you to respond.

As the two of you interact, what is most important to the returning employee is not how they perceive themselves but how they perceive you perceiving them. They are hoping you will accept them and connect with them in their new "self." They are looking for understanding and support.

Here are some of the fears they have about how you will perceive them. These are some of the things they might be saying to themselves about you:

I don't want others to see me get emotionally upset or break down and cry.
I hope they don't think of me as a bad spouse or parent.
What if my co-workers avoid me?
What if they try to pry into my personal life?
I couldn't stand it if they pitied me, felt sorry for me or laughed at me behind my back.
I'm afraid they will see me as a weak person for needing time off.

What does doing the job feel like for the returning TLE employee? Is it easy or hard to perform?

If the returning TLE employee has been absent for only a few days, the readjustment to the job is usually easier than if the absence is much longer. The longer the person is away, the stranger it feels coming back to the workplace. It may be hard to get back into the routine and keep up the pace with everyone. They may fear not meeting your expectations of them.

"Jim came back to work the next day after his doctor told him he had prostate cancer," a phone company manager told me. "The news was pretty shocking, since it came right out of the blue. He was a bit distracted at his job for a few days after the news, but everybody on the team liked him and he knew it. I asked him if he wanted me to keep it quiet or inform his co-workers about the cancer. He said he would tell them himself in his own way. When he did, everyone was very supportive. Knowing that, he was able to work just fine from then on," he said.

If the workplace environment has always felt emotionally safe and inviting—creative assignments, enjoyable co-workers, an understanding manager, and job security—the re-entry should go smoothly and easily, as it did for Jim. If the workplace has not been emotionally safe and inviting, the re-entry may be more difficult.

Andrea was always a troublesome employee. Her manager knew it, her co-workers knew it, and she knew it. She was often on the edge of being fired. She complained a lot to anyone who would listen. It was harder and harder for people in the office to give her the benefit of the doubt. When her husband died suddenly, she remained away from the office for over three weeks. She said she had to get all his financial affairs in order and that he had kept very sloppy records. When she returned to the workplace, she had lots of fears about her place there. She felt quite insecure.

Just as returning employees may have fears about how others perceive them, they also have fears generated by their jobs and the workplace itself. For example, they say to themselves things like:

I'm afraid I will lose, or have already lost, my old job.
I suspect I have already been replaced or they will feel they don't need me at all.
I'm sure the person who covered for me while I was gone did a better job than I ever did.
Even if I have my job back, maybe I won't be able to perform as well as I used to.
Can I live up to expectations?
Will I ever be as fast or effective as I used to be?
Will I have the physical strength to handle my job—or catch up?

What Are the Hardest Things for Trauma Survivors to Face in the Workplace?

For the returning TLE employee the hardest things to face are the other employees and the job. They liked themselves better before the traumatic experience, and they feel sure you did too. That's why they're afraid to face you or they feel insecure about it.

Most traumatized employees believe they were more competent and capable before the trauma, and realize that it's quite obvious that their trauma has had a negative effect on their competency and capability.

Fred was outside the factory driving a forklift, minding his own business, when a fuel line broke and Fred was knocked off his forklift from the impact of the explosion. A few broken ribs and some severe burns put him into the hospital for several days. One of the long-term physical consequences of the accident for Fred was major hearing loss. Being able to hear well was an important part of Fred's job, so one of his biggest fears after returning to work was that he might be incapable of doing his job.

How Long Do the Effects of Trauma Last in the Workplace Situation?

It depends on the nature and severity of the traumatic experience. Obviously, the emotional consequences and other effects of a severe trauma such as a rape, a murder, a kidnapping, a hostage situation or a robbery at gunpoint may last for months and years.

Isabel fell two stories down an open elevator shaft during construction. Luckily, she wasn't killed by the fall. But the accident left her with long-term physical pain, dependency on pain-killing drugs, and an emotional scar about construction areas and elevators. Whenever she hears construction equipment noises or stands in front of an elevator, the memory of her scary fall resurfaces.

Jerry is another example of the lasting effects of a single traumatic experience. One night, when everyone else had gone home and Jerry was last to leave the building, he was mugged right outside the door to the parking lot. He was traumatized by the event. To this day, he is fearful and suspicious, jumpy and anxious in what used to be a non-threatening environment. Nowadays, he is never the last one to leave the plant and often waits at quitting time inside the door for others so that he can walk to the parking lot as part of a group.

After lunch one day, Tanya was walking back to the office. Just as she was about to cross the street, a car turning the corner swerved and hit another car, which hit and killed a pedestrian a few feet in front of her. Had she been a few seconds earlier, the dead pedestrian could have been her. Even though the accident did not happen to her—there was not a scratch on her body—she was traumatized by it. When she walked in the office door, her manager noticed that she looked unusually pale and called her over to talk. He realized that Tanya may have gone into shock, so he sent her to the nurse's office to rest and be cared for. He also told some of her co-workers that she had a traumatic life experience and they should put out a welcome mat for her and let share what had happened to her. Many weeks later, co-workers still noticed about how over-cautious and fearful Tanya was crossing the street, even when they were walking with her.

As Rabbi Harold S. Kushner (1981) comments in his classic book, *When Bad Things Happen to Good People.* After a serious trauma, people are entitled to at least one year of not being their normal selves.

Is re-entry different when the traumatic experience happens at the workplace than when it happens outside or at home?

Yes, very much so. If the traumatic experience happened at home, reminders of the trauma are more likely to be associated with the home environment, though some of the trauma's consequences will be felt in the workplace.

Traumas that happen on the job are different in that the workplace itself was the scene of the traumatic experience. So, every time the traumatized employees return to the workplace, it will remind them of the traumatic event.

Some of these "shared" traumatic experiences include a bomb threat, a rapist somewhere in the building (learning that someone was recently raped in the building), being confronted by a deranged or aggressive person.

"We had a shoot-out in our office," explained a technician. "Two people were killed, and a number of others were injured. I was one of those who got under my desk as soon as I heard the crazy guy shouting in the doorway. When it happened, I had just started my computer and my desktop screen had just come on. To this day, whenever I turn on my computer, I can hear that guy's voice screaming in anger. And instinctively I turn my head to see if anyone is in the doorway."

Another said, "Every time I take this green dress out of my closet to wear it to work, I remember it was the dress I wore the day we had the attacker in our office."

Yet still, "How could I ever forget it? Look, here's a crack in my desk where a bullet hit. Every time I sit down, I am faced with that crack. If I hadn't been in the Ladies Room at the time, I would have taken that bullet instead of my desk."

"Natalie was my best friend, and she was shot to death by that crazy gunman. I keep her picture on my desk to remind me how lucky I am to be alive, and how sad I am that my best friend was killed for no reason at all," said a worker.

When a group of people have all been traumatized together by the same event, they tend to talk about it more and revisit it more often. Many things in the workplace remind them of the trauma.

The office group described above got together and planted a tree near their building to commemorate those who died in the office attack. They stood in a circle around the tree, holding hands. Someone offered a prayer that they might leave all their bad memories of the event outside the building. They also put photos of the two people who were shot to death on the wall near the doorway, to honor their memory. It was their way of putting the negative effects of the traumatic incident behind them so they could go forward with their work in peace.

Psychologists suggest that when a group of people who work together share a traumatic event, they need to ritualize what happened, so they can collectively get closure on the event.

Individually, they also may all need some form of professional psychological treatment for their trauma. Some may need it more than others. But, individual therapy does not replace the need for the employees as a group to ritualize the traumatic event and its consequences.

Do All People in a Workplace React the Same Way to a Trauma that Happens There?

The answer is no. People will react differently depending on their past history of traumatic experience.

For example, five people on a special project team were seated around a conference table, everyone excitedly talking about a major delay confronting them. They wondered how they were going to deal with it and still make their project deadline within budget. Amid all this animated discussion, George, a key technician for the project, had a massive heart attack and died almost instantly, right there in front of the entire team.

Every team member had liked George. They had been working together daily as a team for over a year. No one, including George himself, had known he had a heart condition. Theoretically, every team member should have reacted to the traumatic life experience in the same way and to the same degree. But that did not happen.

Molly was the most seriously traumatized of the group. She had had a similar experience less than a year before, when her father, who was in the best of health, died instantly at the dining room table from an allergic reaction to some food. She had been traumatized by her father's death when it happened with all the family sitting and talking together. George's massive coronary was an almost exact replay of her earlier trauma.

Phil was the next most serious. Ten years ago, he had watched his brother die almost instantly on the street of a bullet wound in a drive-by shooting. George's death wasn't an exact replica of his brother's death, but it was close enough. In fact, he recalled, his brother's death was the first thought that came into his mind when he saw George collapse. Besides, Phil was sitting right next to George at the conference table when it happened.

Psychologists tell us that people with a history of similar traumatic experiences can be affected more powerfully by a similar traumatic experience than someone else might be who had not experienced a similar trauma before.

The others in the group had indeed gone through a traumatic life experience in watching George's death, but they were not seriously traumatized by it. Consequently, they needed less professional psychotherapeutic care than Molly and Phil. The project was put on hold for a few weeks, ostensibly until they could find a replacement for George, but in reality it was because the original project team members were emotionally unable to start up again so soon.

Their manager suggested they find a ritual that the team could carry out to bring closure to George's death for themselves. The team decided to meet once again in the room where George had died and to tell stories about George and the project. Finally, they each said a prayer aloud for George and told the group how they personally would remember him. They also decided informally to name the project after him. Even though it had its technical name, among themselves they called it "George's Project."

Chapter Six

What Does Psychology Tell Us about Trauma?

TLE employees who have been severely traumatized may need to see a professional psychotherapist. Usually, the Employee Assistance Counselor arranges this. Some traumatized persons may also need to be evaluated by a psychiatrist for medication to deal with emotional stress, since only physicians can write prescriptions.

It may be helpful for you as a manager of returning TLE employees to have a picture of what goes on psychologically when a person is traumatized. For example, with a rape victim.

THE TRAUMA OF RAPE

More than once a minute, 78 times an hour, 1,871 times a day, girls and women in America are raped, according to the latest statistics (Bates, 2000). Rape also happens to men and boys, and it is also traumatic for them.

Rape is defined as sexual assault or abuse; sexual intercourse against the will and without the consent of the individual. Legally, rape is also a crime.

For most victims, rape is experienced primarily as an act of violence in which the sexual act is secondary to the brutality of the attack. Many rape cases are not reported by victims because of feelings of shame, guilt, embarrassment, or fear.

Most of all, rape produces a physical and psychological emergency—a TLE of the highest order—and the victim must be treated with compassion as well as professional competence.

Immediately after the crime of rape has occurred victims should be calmed down as much as possible and assured that they are safe (Bahls, 2000). Bleeding wounds, fractures, and other existing injuries should be treated with first aid measures. If victims refuse to seek medical, legal, or psychological help, they have a right to make such a choice, but they should be encouraged to consult a physician as soon as possible. If victims decide to report the crime, they are advised not to change clothes, bathe, douche, or urinate because these actions may destroy legal evidence needed to arrest and convict the attacker (Miller-Keane, 2000).

Psychological recovery from rape is a difficult task. Some victims may appear to return to normal rather quickly, when, in fact, they are using temporary psychological mechanisms such as denial, suppression and rationalization to mask the effects of the trauma. Foa and Rothbaum (1998) *Treating the trauma of rape: Cognitive behavioral therapy for PTSD* suggest that victims may still be in shock up to two weeks after the traumatic event.

Crisis intervention through all phases of the emotional recovery period has always been seen as a necessary component of the total professional care of a rape victim. However, Foa and Rothbaum (1998) report that, to date, there is no well-researched evidence that commonly used crisis interventions have proven effective. Rather, they suggest that trauma victims are better able to benefit from *interventions that process the event later on rather than immediately following the trauma*, especially if the victim is still in shock.

Emotionally, the main purposes of professional follow-ups are to keep the channels of communication open to the victims, to find out how they are doing, to offer support and encouragement in their efforts to resume life, and to provide assistance and referral if necessary (Miller-Keane, 2000). Above all, it is imperative that health care professionals avoid any tendency to moralize or sit in judgment of the victim.

This advice is also well taken for managers and co-workers upon the return to the workplace of a rape-survivor. Be compassionate, provide an emotional safe place and keep channels of communication open. Simply say you know what happened and are very sorry about it, but do not ask for details of the trauma, as the memory of it may, for some time, generate shame, embarrassment, guilt or fear. Above all, avoid any tendency to moralize or sit in judgment of the employee. For a manager or co-worker to suggest or even infer that the victim might have "invited" the rape or "agreed" to it would only exacerbate the trauma's already deleterious effects and hinder recovery.

Most survivors of trauma relive their traumatic experiences over and over again in flashes of memory, and cannot seem to stop themselves from doing it. This causes additional stress in their lives, and can even create a more permanent psychological disorder.

POST TRAUMATIC STRESS DISORDER (PTSD)

Many psychotherapeutic techniques have been used in hopes of reducing the kinds of interruptive flashbacks and other emotional debilitation that traumatized people suffer. Most of these techniques have been studied with traumas that qualify as PTSD (Post-Traumatic Stress Disorder). Much of this research began in earnest after the Vietnam conflict when many veterans who had been in or near violent combat showed the symptoms of PTSD.[1]

Post Traumatic Stress Disorder (PTSD) is described in the *Diagnostic and Statistical Manual of Mental Disorders*, published by the American Psychiatric Association (1980), as an anxiety disorder precipitated by an event [trauma] that falls outside usual human experience and characterized by symptoms of *re-experiencing* (e.g., nightmares, flashbacks), *avoidance and numbing* (e.g., avoidance of reminders, selective amnesia), and *arousal* (e.g., difficulty sleeping, exaggerated startle) that persist longer than one month after the trauma (American Psychiatric Association, 1987). PTSD affects close to 50% of women who have been raped (Rothbaum/Foa et al. 1992). In fact, in one study, 76% of rape victims reported PTSD symptoms at some point within a year after the assault (Resnick, 1989).

After any major trauma, almost all people will experience psychological disturbance. This is normal and most will recover over time, so it is important to distinguish between a normal reaction to trauma and a pathological one that qualifies as PTSD and requires special intervention. For example, the small percentage of rape victims who do not qualify as PTSD are usually diagnosed as falling into a relatively new psychiatric category called *acute stress disorder* (DSM-IV. 1994). The major difference between these two psychiatric categories is not their symptoms but their duration. When symptoms persist beyond one month, a diagnosis of PTSD is appropriate.

For example, ten years after the war, PTSD veterans were still having flashbacks of battle. They might be sitting with a group of friends at a picnic, hear a car backfire or a firecracker go off, and in their minds and imaginations they are back in Vietnam. They are re-living the episode as if it were still happening at this moment. Their bodies cringe in fear. Because the trauma repeatedly and unpredictably interrupts them, even amid daily activities, many could not resume the normal course of their lives. For some, "it's as if time had stopped at the moment of the trauma."[2]

With the rise of the women's movement in the 1960s, therapists began to notice that rape victims and women living in severe abusive situations also manifested PTSD symptoms. Only in the 1970s, Judith Lewis Herman (1992) wrote, *Trauma and Recovery* was it recognized that the most common forms of post traumatic stress disorders are not those of men in war but of women in civilian life."[3] But it was only in the next decade that psychologists and the courts recognized that traumatic events like rape and other violent acts were not simply single events, but experiences that produced extended physical, mental and emotional consequences in the victim. Survivors reported bouts of insomnia, nausea, nightmares, dissociation, numbness and startle responses for weeks and months after the traumatic experience.

One rape survivor wrote, "I was terrified to go anywhere on my own. . . I felt too defenseless and too afraid, and so I just stopped doing anything. . . I would just stay home and I was just frightened."[4]

Today, a much wider spectrum of traumatic experiences are being classified as PTSD—people witnessing a cruel murder firsthand, people involved in major auto accidents, people held hostage, people affected by an explosion or trapped in a burning building, people witnessing the sudden death of a loved one when it was not anticipated, and many others. All of these survivors manifest many of the physical, mental and emotional consequences of military combat trauma or rape as well as a memory processing system that was short-circuited.

THE WAY MEMORY WORKS

Normally, when events occur in our lives, whether they are important or unimportant, a number of standard steps are taken automatically in our brains, where memories are processed and stored. Typically, when an event first occurs, it is registered as an "episode" of sensory and emotional details in the limbic system of the brain, specifically in a certain area of the hippocampus (Schore, 2000). An episodic memory is as yet unconnected and unassociated with the rest of our lives or our activities. Think of an episodic memory as a package dropped at your doorstep by a delivery person. You don't yet know who it is for or where it will be placed in your house. At this point, it is just an incomplete process—a package on your doorstep. The package needs to be opened, identified and given meaning. The same needs to happen to any event that is held only in its episodic form in your limbic brain. At that point, it is merely a bundle of sensations and feelings just waiting at the brain's memory doorstep.

Normally, according to van der Kolk (1985), details of the episodic memory are carried almost immediately from the hippocampus to the prefrontal area of your neocortex, the thinking part of your brain, somewhere behind your eyes. There, the sensory and emotional details from the event are extracted, abstracted and formed into a story. The event is given meaning, significance and even ethical perspective for you. The memory gets logged in, as it were, with a date and time stamped on it; it becomes a part of your history. It is put into its temporal-spatial context. There, at the same time it is also associated with other things that are currently happening—the clothes you are wearing, the others who are present, etc.—to form a fuller story.

Technically, in this cerebral location, the episodic memory is given what brain researchers call a "semantic meaning," and, in moments, it is sent back to another area of the hippocampus to be stored as a regular memory, able to be recalled when needed (Bergmann, 2000).[5] This is what happens with the memory of a *normal* event.

For example, if I go to a concert and have a great time, I remember not only the concert, but also all the details surrounding the event—what I was wearing, who was with me, what we had to eat and drink, what we did afterwards. My brain gives the event a semantic meaning and locates it in my history. From then on, I can remember the date and time when it happened, and I can look back upon it and locate it among other events in my life.

Some memories are of special importance to us. For example, if you ask people where they were at the time of President Kennedy's assassination or when the space shuttle Challenger blew up or when the World Trade Center was blown up, most people can remember. This means these are very important semantic memories.

SHORT-CIRCUITED MEMORY PROCESS

According to Bergmann (2000) something different happens—or rather *doesn't* happen—when a traumatic event occurs. Immediately after the traumatic experience, we observe that the traumatized person may go into shock. Such persons may feel stunned, startled, helpless, and defenseless to fight off or flee from the overwhelming event. They are often disoriented. When you ask them later on, what they did or said immediately after the traumatic event, they often cannot remember.

Brain researchers tell us that in cases like these, the normal memory cycle in the brain gets short-circuited. The event is registered as an episodic memory, the first step in the memory cycle, but the process stops there. Such traumatic events never get their semantic meanings. Traumatic events, especially powerful ones, never get beyond episodic memory. This means the traumatic event is not tied to any time and place in the person's history; it has no context in the survivor's life. So, the episodic traumatic memory can burst out and replay itself randomly over and over as if it were always happening for the first time.

When an episodic memory replays itself, it seems real and immediate, even though, in fact, it may have happened weeks, months, or even years ago. Such spontaneous recurrences of the traumatic episode are called "flashbacks." When these replays happen during ordinary activities, such as at work, they disorient the person having them, for they reactivate the trauma. It is usually quite obvious when a person is having a flashback in a workplace setting such as at meetings or when a team is together, because the trauma survivor may go blank or may be unsuspectingly flooded with images of the trauma and emotions associated with it. The survivor apparently has no power to stop these images and emotions, and is overwhelmed once again by an event that happened in the past.

SOLVING AN OLD DILEMMA

This short-circuited memory processing that happens in trauma has been recognized for more than a century. In 1889, the French physician Pierre Janet wrote a major work on psychological trauma. Using careful research, including hypnosis, Janet showed that traumatic memories were preserved in "an abnormal state, set apart from ordinary consciousness." He believed that the intense emotional reaction to traumatic experiences severed the normal connections of memory, knowledge and emotion. Such intense emotion, he wrote, incapacitated the synthesizing function of the mind.[6]

Janet had to come to these insightful conclusions through inference, for he had no way of looking at the brain directly or watching its activity as we do today. It is only in our era of highly sophisticated methods of brain scanning that we can light up different parts of the brain, so to speak, and verify these cerebral locations, pathways and processes—and recognize the way trauma incapacitates the synthesizing function of the mind.

MAKING A TRAUMATIC MEMORY A NORMAL MEMORY

The best hope for full recovery and psychological healing from trauma seems to happen only after the episodic memory, stuck in one area of the hippocampus, can complete its natural cycle, be given semantic meaning in the prefrontal cortex, and be returned to another area of the hippocampus as a normal memory. Once the traumatic event completes the normal memory cycle, the person can recall the event without re-experiencing it with all its overwhelming emotion. Such a person can remember that the event happened in their personal history at a certain time and place, and belongs in the past. They know, for the first time perhaps, that the trauma is not happening now.

CATEGORIES OF INTERVENTION

There are three general categories of intervention for PTSD in general and other traumatic life experiences.

The first category is *psychosocial* and include (1) hypnotherapy, (2) psychodynamic psychotherapy and (3) group therapy. Since at least the time of Freud, hypnosis has continued to be used in treating trauma victims in order to resolve the psychic conflict (Spiegel, 1989). Dynamic psychotherapists in treating traumatized victims emphasize concepts such as denial, abreaction and catharsis and have outlined stages of recovery from trauma (Horowitz, 1986, 2, 1994); however, psychoanalytically oriented therapy has not proven very successful (Bart, 1975). Apparently, these approaches, especially with clients with PTSD symptoms, are not generally effective in transforming the episodic memory of the trauma into a normal memory.

Other psychodynamic approaches focus primarily on group process (Yalom, 1995) but they have not been widely tested. PTSD combat veterans discovered that getting together in group therapy sessions, telling one another their trauma stories, seemed to be more helpful than one-on-one classical psychotherapy.

Managers and co-workers can encourage returning TLE employees to take advantage of whatever professional help they can get, and to stay with it, even though it doesn't seem to be immediately helpful. If there are informal support groups available—and there usually are, from cancer survivor support groups to pet loss support groups—encourage trauma survivors to participate in them. Many people find them comforting, supportive and healing.

The second category is *pharmacological* interventions. Medication has been used for over 100 years to alleviate distress following trauma. Currently, these approaches to the trauma of rape advocate the use of medications either (1) to *reactivate* the traumatic experience as a means to help uncover repressed or dissociated material or, in complete contrast, (2) to *suppress* symptoms that are disrupting victims' lives, allowing them to restore their normal effective coping mechanisms (Sargent and Slater, 1940). Using medications with traumatized persons is based on the evidence that traumatic events leave their imprint on the victim's limbic brain circuitry, autonomic nervous system, and arousal systems, and that drugs can help restore proper brain and memory functioning. The return to medication is also in response to the research showing that traditional psychotherapy has little or no affect in re-establishing normalcy after such imprinting (ver Ellen and van Kammen, 1990).

Managers and co-workers should be aware that many pharmaceutical drug interventions for trauma victims can have an effect on the returning TLE employee's ability to perform certain jobs. For example, many medications today have warnings that persons while under their influence should not drive a car or operate dangerous machinery. When a returning employee has such a job, you might ask: "Do you happen to be taking any medications that are meant to calm and relax you? If so, I don't want you to be in any danger of getting hurt. Perhaps, we can shift some of your responsibilities for a while?"

COGNITIVE-BEHAVIORAL APPROACHES

The third category, the most rigorously researched, are the *cognitive-behavioral* approaches. Among this category are one set of approaches called *anxiety management training* (AMT), which includes techniques such as (1) stress inoculation training, (2) thought-stopping and (3) cognitive restructuring (see Foa et. al. 1998). These techniques to foster recovery from trauma are based on the belief that the victims feel pathological anxiety because they are deficient in personal coping skills (Suinn, 1974). AMT techniques include relaxation training, positive self-statements, breathing retraining, biofeedback, social skills training, and distraction methods. Thus, the aim of AMT is to furnish clients with ways to manage anxiety when it occurs. They are akin to the pharmacological approaches that use medication to suppress disruptive symptoms following the trauma.

Another set of approaches in this cognitive-behavioral category are called *exposure techniques* such as (1) systematic desensitization, (2) other imaginal and *in vivo* exposure treatments such as prolonged exposure (PE), and (3) eye movement desensitization and reprocessing (EMDR). In contrast to AMT techniques whose purpose is to reduce anxiety and take the client's mind off the traumatic event, these approaches take an opposite tack and seek to activate trauma memories—much as the reactivating pharmacological approaches attempt to do. Their underlying assumption is that by exposing and confronting the feared situation they can help the victim modify pathological aspects of these memories. According to Foa and Rothbaum (1998), exposure techniques have proven to be the most effective, the most efficient, and the most user-friendly.

In *systematic desensitization*, the therapist uses pairs of short events (an image of the fearful experience combined with relaxation) in a graded sequence

beginning with the least distressing scenario. Thus, systematically, the client
is able to confront scenarios that are more and more frightening, culminating
in being able to confront an imaginal image of the original trauma (Frank et
al., 1988).

Other *imaginal exposure treatments* found that pairing "relaxation" with
the fearful stimuli, as was done in the systematic desensitization approach,
was unnecessary. Instead, they use a variety of imaginal and *in vivo* (real
life) exposure techniques, which promote the experience of anxiety during confrontation with the feared situation or image (Johnson et al., 1982).
In this approach, the therapist might show the survivor photographs of the
trauma setting—for example, the place where the rape was initiated—and
eventually accompany the survivor to the physical location itself. *Prolonged
exposure* (PE) is one of these techniques. Its program begins with breathing
retraining, and then focuses on exposing the client in reality (*in vivo*) to the
feared situation plus repeated reliving of the trauma in imagination. In their
book, *Treating the Trauma of Rape*, Foa and Rothbaum (1998) find PE to be
the treatment of choice for rape victims who meet PTSD criteria. Other approaches or various combinations of the above that favor desensitization of
the memory have been tried.

Again, managers and co-workers should encourage returning TLE employees to take advantage of any professional help that is readily available, and to
keep using it as long as it proves helpful.

EYE MOVEMENT DESENSITIZATION REPROCESSING (EMDR)

More recently, a rather simple technique of bilateral stimulation of the brain
while the survivor is recalling the traumatic event seems able, simply and directly, to help the brain complete the normal memory process. The process is
called EMDR (Shapiro, 1995). Apparently, such bilateral stimulation allows
the brain to take the episodic memory up to the cortex, give it a semantic meaning there, and return it to the hippocampus as a normal memory (van der Kolk
et al., 1985, Schore, 2000). After EMDR, the traumatic event is stored like any
other memory, in its historical context. And the flashbacks disappear.

Originally, this bilateral stimulation was done by the therapist waving a
finger back and forth in front of the client's eyes, asking the client to track
the finger movement with her eyes. Thus the name "eye movement" desensitization. Today, the bilateral brain stimulation may be accomplished using
a variety of modes, for example, by alternately tapping the client's left and
right shoulders (Parnell, 1997). The bilateral stimulation process is repeated
until anxiety decreases.

An EMDR treatment does not end merely with a reduction of anxiety. Its bilateral stimulation may also be used to help victims come to a realistically positive view of themselves. Instead of still seeing themselves as either dirty, guilty, shameful, damaged or bad, they are encouraged to view themselves as survivors, as persons who are courageous, resourceful and strong. This EMDR process is referred to as "installing a positive cognition" (Parnell, 1997).

Managers and co-workers can support any returning TLE employees who are seeking EMDR. Those certified to do EMDR are almost always people licensed in a mental health profession.

HEALING TRAUMA USING THE BODY'S SENSATIONS

While most therapists traditionally regard posttraumatic stress as a disorder of the mind and use mental or mind-altering pharmaceuticals to treat it, there are others who claim that trauma can be healed only by a treatment that integrates body and mind. While talk therapy and drugs can be helpful, and at times essential, writes Peter A. Levine (1997) in *Waking the Tiger: Healing Trauma,* "trauma is not, will not, and can never be fully healed until we also address the essential role played by the body. We must understand how the body is affected by trauma and its central position in its aftermath"[7] (p. 3).

This approach is based on the fact that the body itself reacts profoundly to a traumatic experience. Just as the mind protects itself from being overwhelmed, so does the body. For example, the body may tense its muscles, shake in fear, freeze in terror or collapse and shut itself off when overwhelmed. Just as mental treatments are designed to normalize the mind's activity after the event, the body's responses are meant to be normalized after the event, and if this somatic process goes unrecognized and untreated, the trauma can never be fully healed. "Somatic Experiencing," is a well-integrated body-mind process developed by Peter Levine and based on the "felt sense" concept coined by Eugene Gendlin (1978) in his book *Focusing.* In these body-centered approaches, "Body sensation, rather than intense emotion, is the key to healing trauma," claims Levine.[8] However, these approaches are relatively new and have not been the subject of much scientific research. Nevertheless, they will undoubtedly become more recognized.

A WORD TO MANAGERS

Although the suggestions given to managers and co-workers in dealing with returning TLE employees do not in themselves change the episodic memory

to a normal one heal the trauma or remove its unwelcome physical consequences, they do provide an important *context* for the emotional recovery
process to take place. In other words, what managers and co-workers can
do does not replace any necessary professional therapeutic work, but it does
make a significant contribution.

Put out a welcome mat. Since the TLE employee typically feels unsure, insecure, anxious and upset after the traumatic event, managers and co-workers
creating a safe context in the workplace for the returning employee form an
essential context for successful and timely recovery. The fact is that a therapist can create a safe context for the survivor only for the length of a therapy
session. In contrast, managers and co-workers can create a safe place for the
length of a workday, every workday.

Lend a listening ear. Since the traumatic event itself remains prominent
in the survivor's consciousness while understanding the emotional recovery
process is taking place, managers and co-workers open to the survivor's retelling of the trauma story and their experience offers temporary relief to the
sometimes confused and dissociated employee.

Offer a helping hand. Traumatic events themselves change the persons
who undergo them so that former personal connections and relationships feel
lost or broken. Therefore, managers and co-workers who help restore connections to the returning TLE employee and the workplace are cooperating in the
emotional recovery process in a way that a therapist or a therapy group cannot do. The therapist cannot re-establish the patient's mental and emotional
connections with significant people in the patient's life. Only the patient and
those significant people can do that. For most people especially traumatized
employees, their workplace is a major source of community, so re-establishing connections with managers and fellow workers is something only those
employees can do. And it is often they who must initiate the helping hand.

NOTES

1. The first formal recognition of PTSD as an official diagnosis did not occur in
the American Psychiatric Association's manual of mental disorders (DSM-III-R)
until 1980.

2. *Trauma and Recovery: The Aftermath of Violence-from domestic abuse to political terror.* (New York: Basic Books, 1992, p. 37.

3. *Ibid.,* p. 28.

4. *Quoted in Rape: The First Sourcebook for Women,* ed. N. Connell and C. Wilson. (New York: New American Library, 1974) p. 44.

5. Many other parts of the brain, such as the amygdala, medulla, pons and cerebellum as well as many chemical neutrotransmitters, are involved in the brain's com-

plex system for processing memories, but for our purposes this simplified version is enough.

6. P. Janet, *L'Automatisme Psychologique.* Paris: Felix Alcan, 1889, p. 457. Janet's research was mainly with women traumatized by rape and incest. Fifty years after Janet, working with victims of combat trauma after World War II, Abraham Kardiner came to much the same conclusion.

7. *Waking the Tiger: Healing Trauma.* (Berkley, California: North Atlantic Books, 1997), p. 3.

8. *Focusing.* (New York: Bantam Books, 19978), p. 10.

Chapter Seven

What Can an Employee Assistance Program Do?

WHAT IS AN EMPLOYEE ASSISTANCE PROGRAM (EAP)?

Everyone knows that when people feel good, they tend to work well. Unfortunately, there are things that occur that can traumatize employees. Some of these deeply upsetting experiences happen on the job, but many don't have anything to do with the workplace. Regardless of what can traumatize an employee, the negative feelings—fear, confusion, embarrassment, anger, distrust, shame, irritability, anxiety, worries—of one person can easily affect an entire work group. And this is where an Employee Assistance Program (EAP) comes in, for it can help employees resolve certain problems.

Most government agencies and large companies have an Employee Assistance Program, to whose counselor's managers may refer employees who have had a traumatic life experience. Managers should ensure that a TLE employee gets to see a counselor.

However, since most employees have not used EAP services in this way, managers should reassure the TLE employee that the company wants to provide whatever help may be needed in the employee's recovery. For example, if the traumatic experience was being fired, the EAP may help in a job search. If the problem is alcoholism or other substance abuse, EAP may assist in finding a local group or a residential program if needed. Managers may communicate the message that the company wants you to be healthy and that the company is proud of its employees who are courageous enough to want to be healthy and productive.

Explain to the employee that there is no stigma attached to seeing an EAP counselor, which it is not a problem with the department or office either. Almost everyone is likely, at one time or another, to have situations come up where they need help in resolving something in their work environment.

In addition to traumatic life experiences, the reasons employees seek help from EAP specialist in their companies are many and varied. Some may come for help in career counseling, job relocation, stress management or conflict resolution. Many have financial questions about company benefits, retirement programs, union regulations, and payroll deductions. Others may face difficulty in areas of their home life and need help with preventive healthcare, diet and nutrition, parenting, adoption, childcare, and deadbeat spouses. Still others file grievances in the workplace dealing with co-worker bullies, control-freak bosses, sexual harassment, and abusive managers, alcohol-dependent or drug-using colleagues.

Human resource people recognize that employees often confront personal problems that can negatively impact their work performance. The aim of an EAP is to help the troubled person's search for solutions to problems and return the employee to his or her best level of workplace performance.

A well-designed Employee Assistance Program is cost effective. It can increase productivity, make managing easier, reduce absenteeism, and reduce attrition. Companies can't afford to lose good employees these days, because the estimated cost to a company for each person replaced, according to social worker Mark Gorkin, is equal to at least one year's salary for that individual.

THE GROWTH OF EMPLOYEE ASSISTANCE PROGRAMS

The Employee Assistance Program has changed and grown since the first "Occupational Alcohol Program" of the 1940s. The range of services provided by today's EAP professionals has broadened to include marriage and family problems, stress related problems, financial and legal difficulties, and psychological and workplace conflict. In fact, the website for the University of Texas Southwestern Medical Center's EAP program opens with this poster, indicating the incredible spread of issues dealt with by today's EAP professionals in large organizations and corporations.

DO ANY OF THESE APPLY TO YOU OR YOUR FAMILY?

Family Problems
Single Parenting
Dual Careers
Anxiety
Depression

Parent/Child Conflict
Job "Burnout"
Work Related Problems
Divorce
Career Change
Financial Pressures
Physical Abuse
Interpersonal Communication
Alcohol or Drug Problems
Life Transition
Aging Parents
Unresolved Grief
Marital Problems
Sexual Problems
Personal Concerns
Problems of Adolescence
Stress
Relationship Problems
Eating Disorders
Legal Issues

EAP professional counselors in organizations today provide confidential assessment and short-term counseling to employees and their families to help them deal with any or all of these issues.

The number of government agencies and companies supporting EAP programs has also increased substantially. The business community has recognized that many everyday life stresses can negatively affect employee attendance and concentration, general workplace morale, and an employee's ability to perform well on the job. Today, many companies have even increased EAP services for their employees because they can measure the results in productivity and profits. For example, the American Mental Health Association estimates that 10% to 15% of employees have severe personal problems. If 5% of a company's employees used the EAP, the potential monetary savings would be 3.45% of payroll for reduced absenteeism and improved productivity from problem employees. Companies with EAP services typically have about 75% reduction in inpatient alcohol and other drug abuse treatment costs, about 17% fewer accidents, about 35% reduced turnover, about 21% lower absenteeism, and about 14% higher productivity.

Typically, EAP staff members are culturally diverse and highly credentialed. Almost all are licensed for independent therapeutic practice and hold recognized certifications. Depending on location, they may be Licensed

Clinical Social Workers (LCSW), psychologists, psychiatrists and experienced EAP and Substance Abuse Professionals (SAP). They will have varied experience in many aspects of diagnostic assessment, counseling, crisis intervention, and referral to community resources. As a rule, they are also highly experienced in training, supervisory/management consultation and work-group dynamics. There is also available a credential, the CEAP, or Certified Employee Assistance Professional, designed specifically for the EAP profession.

Companies too small to afford their own employee assistance professionals can become affiliated with nationwide EAP centers, each with its full retinue of counselors, social workers, trainers and other specialists in employee problems.

EAP'S CRISIS RESPONSE

What is of concern to this book is the crisis response provided by a company's employee assistance programs. Most recognize that a crisis or traumatic incident is an event that is typically unexpected, sudden and overwhelming for those exposed to it. Some of these terrible events happen in the workplace, such as witnessing a suicide, the violent death of a co-worker, work site accidents involving serious injury or death, or even unexpected violent reactions of an employee being fired.

In an article "Seeking Solutions to Violence on the Job" (1994), Marc T. Braverman, a pioneer in the field of traumatic stress in the workplace, says firings and layoffs as a result of corporate downsizing and restructuring heighten the risk of workplace violence as more employees face the humiliation of fear and rage associated with job loss. Employees who have been fired, demoted or passed over for a promotion may return to the workplace wanting revenge. Because of the employee's despair, he becomes a threat to other employees.

Incidents that illustrate this include the 1991 murders at the U.S. Postal Service in Royal Oak, Michigan, and the 1993 shooting of eight people at the San Francisco law firm of Pettit and Martin (LLC). Braverman stresses the need to look at today's workplace violence issues as "health problems."

According to figures obtained from the National Institute of Occupational Safety and Health (NIOSH) and the Bureau of Statistics, people at work, are often exposed to lethal violence. For example, homicide accounts for 17% of all deaths in the workplace. Research suggests that human resources staff play a most significant role, especially in advising management how to understand and deal with today's organizational problems. This suggests that human resource management needs to reassess and look closely at how the whole organization is communicating with employees and managing them.

Other traumatic events, even though they may happen outside the workplace, have a strong impact on the productive effectiveness of those traumatized by them. In these cases, the goal of the EAP is to put the person in touch with the proper healthcare professionals to debrief the traumatized person as soon as possible and see that they receive further therapeutic care, as needed.

Typically, a traumatized person requires more than a debriefing. Some need weeks and months of therapy. As I have pointed out before, therapists can do only so much for a traumatized person, since they see the client only one hour at a time usually once a week. If the TLE survivor has returned to the workplace, the person's manager and co-workers who see the survivor for eight hours every workday have the opportunity of supporting or destabilizing the work of the professional therapist.

It is surprising how many managers and other employees presume that the job of helping a person recover from a traumatic life experience belongs solely to the EAP professionals of an organization. A further false assumption managers make is that when the TLE employee returns to the job, "all that other emotional stuff" has been taken care of. The fact is it hasn't. The emotional stuff is still there affecting not only the survivor but also the whole team.

A CASE STUDY

I am continually amazed at how unsophisticated our organizations are in understanding and dealing with individuals who have experienced a traumatic life experience (TLE) and are making a re-entry to the workplace. My purpose is to provide a clear and accurate look at the behavior of managers and employees in dealing with traumatized employees in today's organizational settings.

The organization from which this case study is taken is one of the largest government agencies in Washington, DC. However, I find it is no different from any other organization where people are concerned with serving their constituents and customers.

Stanton Stone is a middle manager in the Division of Personnel. He is one of 15 employees who manage a large segment of this agency. He has amassed a total of 32 years of government service, including service in the Air Force. In his late 50's, he is tall with grayish hair and can be described as Anglo. To his peers he is a walking encyclopedia of historical knowledge within the agency. He is respected by his colleagues and all those who have worked with him. He has received numerous awards. He enjoys the camaraderie of senior management officials in the agency, since he is frequently called upon to brief them in his areas of personnel expertise.

In all his years of work, except for an occasional cold, flu or sinus condition, Stanton rarely complained of any serious physical ailments. However, two-and-a-half years ago, Stanton suffered a heart attack at his home in Vienna, Virginia. On a Saturday afternoon while gardening he felt pains in his chest. Rushed to the hospital, he was diagnosed for bypass surgery within a few days. Stanton was out of work for ten weeks following his surgery. His government health plan covered all his hospital, physician and physical therapy expenses.

When he talked about his life before the trauma, he said that his work world had revolved around preparation for hearings on Capitol Hill and buy-out legislation. His calendar was always filled with appointments and meetings. The trauma was an emotional shock, because for three months he played no part in the organization. His life was devoid of all the usual wonderful excitement and challenge.

Moreover, he said, he had always been an independent person, but after the trauma he had to become dependent, both physically and mentally. His recuperation from surgery fell hard on him and his family. His two teenage children were afraid he might die. He kept trying to reassure them that everything was going to be all right. He said his wife had to make the biggest transition in learning to pay bills and maintaining the household, things he had done for 25 years. Stanton said, "Although I had little to do and few responsibilities, it was a very stressful time."

His convalescence took longer than expected because minor complications set in after the surgery. He experienced sporadic pain in his back and was diagnosed as having sleep apnea.

When I asked Stanton what his superiors had done for him during his recuperation period, I expected him to mention things like, they saw that I got counseling, they came for personal visits, and they found ways of staying connected to me. But none of these gestures of human care had happened.

When he returned to work, he experienced a real dichotomy between the response of his colleagues and that of upper management. His colleagues, he said, were interested in what had happened to him; they were supportive and assured him they would be there for him if he needed anything.

In contrast, managers and senior staff who came by to say hello to him stayed in his cubicle "all of eight seconds." They were not unkind, he acknowledged, but neither did they show an interest in his condition or how he was faring as he re-entered the work community. As Stanton explained, "They just left all that to me. Basically, over time, I found it very frustrating. They really had no interest in how I was doing. I was left alone to drift through the process of re-entry and cope with it as best I could." He explained, "After a long absence of not being on the job, you re-enter the workplace. You are the focus of attention for all your colleagues. And you are not sure of yourself. You feel out of control."

From his own experience he observed, "Physical recovery may take less time than emotional recovery, but emotional recovery is just as important even if it takes a longer time."

Because he had to drive a number of miles in rush hour traffic to get to the office each day, he became fatigued easily. Gradually, he negotiated with his supervisors to work three days at the office and two days at home, mainly because of his continued back pain, fatigue and the long commute. He says this arrangement worked. With regard to productivity, management was willing to provide him with any computer technology he needed to do his job, but they offered him nothing emotionally.

STANTON AND TED

Prior to Stanton's heart bypass surgery he had supervised an employee named Ted, a professional personnel specialist who worked mostly in classification and compensation. At 50 years old, Ted was generally in good health. Soon after Stanton came to this division, Ted was scheduled for brain tumor surgery at Johns Hopkins University Hospital in Baltimore, Maryland. The surgery was classified as experimental, because it involved new procedures.

In learning of this new and untried surgery, Stanton found it very scary. A tumor had been found in Ted's pituitary gland, and to remove it the surgeon would have to go into the center of the brain using a laser procedure. The operation was reported a success. When Ted returned to work, there was no apparent disability or lack of ability to do his job, and he picked up rather quickly. But Stanton said he noticed that Ted wanted to continually talk about his brain tumor and surgery. He would volunteer this information to anyone who would listen. He might stop one of his colleagues and go into a long description of the specifics of his surgery, explaining certain details of his experience, for example, how he lost his sense of taste and smell or how he remembered smelling burning flesh during the operation. Naturally, some co-workers found this very unpleasant and felt embarrassed or annoyed. Some would avoid Ted. Stanton referred him to the employee assistance program for counseling, which Ted appreciated.

After a while Ted had a relapse. He suffered a small stroke and lost his memory. When he returned to work again, he had only a short attention span. Ted was aware of this, and when someone approached him about it, he became defensive. Again, Stanton referred him to EAP for personal therapy.

As his supervisor, Stanton stated, "Ted was able to do his work but I was not sure of my role as manager. I really didn't feel that I knew what I should be doing or not doing. I had no idea how to help him deal with the situation. I certainly felt that I wasn't really prepared. No one in the EAP ever came to me to tell me how I might be helpful in Ted's recovery or what I should tell Ted's co-workers about relating to him."

STANTON'S DILEMMA AS A MANAGER

As organizations are continually challenged to deal with traumatized employees, managers feel they lack the necessary skills to understand what the traumatized person needs when they return to the work place. As I talked with Stanton about his experience in relating to Ted, he said, "Knowing what I know now, both from my own experience and the experience with Ted and some other employees who have had traumatic experiences, I wish I had, first of all, a structured and specific plan about how to relate to them before they come back."

He said, "Next, I would like to be more sensitive to the returning employee. I would like to be able to explore with them how they were feeling as they returned to the workplace, what amount of work they felt capable of doing at the time, and what their concerns were in getting their jobs done. Ted never gave me the opportunity to talk in a private setting. I fault myself for not taking the initiative. I took the easy way out and let him volunteer information, instead of helping him talk about his feelings in a safe environment."

Stanton and I talked about what employees go through when they have traumatic life experiences, especially when they lose their jobs, and what managers think and feel who have to deal with such people. Stanton had strong feelings on this subject. He believed "upper management gives only lip service and very sporadic communication about traumatized employees, leaving immediate supervisors, co-workers and returning workers to shift for themselves."

TED'S DILEMMA AS AN EMPLOYEE

When I was able to hear Ted's side of the story, I discovered he felt very ambivalent coming back to the workplace after his trauma. On the one hand, he felt helpless to tell people what he needed; on the other the hand Stanton, his manager, and the organization in general were at a loss as to how to approach him. The trauma Ted experienced was unusual because it affected his mental capabilities, and he was afraid he would not be able to function as well intellectually as he had before. Because of this, he felt frightened and embarrassed to face anyone. He did not know how much to ask of his manager or the organization, and he did not know how to ask. He felt stranded and unable to define what he needed.

Executives and management in organizations tend to minimize the impact of a trauma on an employee. Co-workers are unsure of how to behave and often purposely avoid talking to the re-entry employee, behaving as though the trauma had never occurred. In most organizations, the current workplace atmosphere is not a healthy situation for the survivor, co-workers or the manager of the group.

Stanton agreed. "Returning employees here," he said, "have not been dealt with in any sensitive manner. Little is done to let them express their concerns or feelings. It certainly is a bad situation that has an impact on productivity and people's motivation."

Now that Stanton had gone through a trauma himself, he felt he would be more sensitive to a re-entry person's needs. If needed, he said, he would search out a close friend of the TLE employee to get information, or go to the employee assistance office and "ask them to tell me how I can help the person. I would find a way to be helpful."

During his interview with me, he would stop talking at times and just stare into space, perhaps recalling his first days back on the job. He repeatedly said that no senior managers reached out to help him. "People were superficially reassuring, but I felt no depth to their feelings." Then, he said, "I would like to know how to make it easier for the re-entry person."

THE BENEFITS OF KNOWLEDGE

To be helpful and not harmful to the emotional recovery process, managers and co-workers will need to learn new skills with a focus on knowing how to communicate well, engage in interpersonal dialogue, and refer employees to appropriate human resources and healthcare services. The Study Circle format, which I discuss in, detail in Part II of this book, provides a simple and easy way to gain much of this knowledge.

Learning these skills is also good business. Caring communication between a manager and an employee upon their re-entry after a trauma can derail a possible grievance or Equal Employment Opportunity (EEO) complaint. For example, the manager who takes the time to openly approach and talk to a returning TLE employee is not only assisting the employee's return but re-establishing the manager's credibility with the employee as a trusting and compassionate person. A manager who continues to create such a caring atmosphere over the long term can diffuse the anger of a TLE employee and help him or her reappraise a difficult situation more positively.

Unfortunately, today's managers are not given policy guidelines or an organizational format for dealing with employees who are returning to the workplace after experiencing a trauma. Survivor's who return need a consciously designed emotional framework that will facilitate and support their re-entry. Hopefully, organizations will begin to recognize this need *as an opportunity*, and will begin to support an intervention designed to create an ambiance that reaches out to returning TLE employees without emotionally harming them.

Long working hours and demanding deadlines create an environment for competitiveness in performance. Without sensitivity toward the returning TLE employee, performance problems can arise or increase, creating another layer of communication hurdles for a manager. The human resource department together with the organization can work together, through appropriate education, to reach out to TLE employees who must find their way through a necessary process of healing and emotional recovery.

The Study Circle on understanding the emotional recovery of trauma for managers and employees provides a simple, not very time-consuming way to educate people in an office about what to expect from employees returning to the workplace after a traumatic life experience. As an educational tool, the Study Circle does not replace the employee's likely need for private counseling or group therapy. Nor does it teach the manager how to deal with the employee's emotional problems the way a therapist would. It does, however, educate managers about three critical areas in the re-entry process: the successive stages most trauma survivors go through in their emotional recovery, how these survivors are likely to behave when they first return to work, and the workplace context of safety and support survivors will need to make the transition smoothly and effectively.

The Study Circle for managers and co-workers brings them new knowledge that can generate powerful though hard-to-quantify benefits. With such education, managers and, with coaching, co-workers can learn to feel more confident in how they respond to a returning TLE employee. When survivors return to a workplace that provides a safe haven for them, a willing ear to listen to their trauma experience, and a helping hand to re-establish connections to the workplace family, they are more likely to recover more quickly and become once again fully productive members of the workplace team.

Trauma and its effects cover every facet of our lives from childhood to adulthood, from birth to death. Understanding it will help many cope on the road to recovery from a traumatic event.

The next phase to address how managers and co-workers can learn to intervene helpfully with a TLE employee by defining effective techniques for reintegrating trauma survivors. For that we need to understand the dynamics of the Study Circle.

Part II

TAKING PRACTICAL STEPS

Chapter Eight

What Is a Study Circle?

INTRODUCTION

A Study Circle is an adult learning format with a wide range of applications. In general, it is designed for participants who lack information in a certain area. It is especially useful in helping a small group of people going through a similar life transition or in coping with an important situation in which they are all invested. For this reason, Study Circles may be used in many different areas of life and to cope with many different issues, not merely dealing with traumatic life experiences.

For example, one Study Circle might involve a group of parents all struggling to cope with their hyperactive children. Another might bring together a group of citizens trying to grasp the implications of an amendment on the voting ballot. A professor or student might occupy a group interested in appreciating poetry or learning a foreign language. A church community may want to create a group of people trying to apply scriptural writings to their lives. Concerned citizens could gather a group of concerned farmers exploring the pros and cons of genetically altered crops. The workplace may want to learn ways to resist sexual harassment in the office. For us, the Study Circle topic is how to deal with employees returning to the workplace after a traumatic life experience (TLE).

The Study Circle may also be used as a tool for enrichment and as a tool to affect change, as with the Study Circle on understanding the emotional recovery of trauma.

I selected the Study Circle method of intervention for dealing with trauma in the workplace because it allows managers and employees to come together to share their views and focus on this specific topic. Study Circles promote both group interaction and collective sharing of ideas and information among participants. In a Study Circle, all individual views are considered, and participants have an opportunity to listen, dialogue and disagree.

A study circle is a democratic form of group learning, where five to fifteen people with a common interest gather to investigate a particular topic. Some topics require few sessions, others require more. The Study Circle on workplace trauma needs three sessions.

Working together, participants learn from each other, from prepared materials and from outside sources. One handout page was all we needed for each session of the Study Circle on workplace trauma. It contained a few definitions and some questions for discussion. No instructor teaches or controls the circle. Led by a facilitator trained in group dynamics and the Study Circle concept, the participants learn from each other's knowledge and experience.

The Study Circle format calls for a facilitator who can give the group members focus, foster discussion, and encourage everyone's ownership of the topic. The facilitator does not teach and need not be an expert in the subject under discussion, but must be familiar enough with the topic to raise questions for the group. The facilitator helps create and maintain a collaborative learning atmosphere where each participant feels free to express ideas, relate personal experiences, and discuss points of view on the subject. A successful facilitator will be a good listener, who quickly gets to know the members, gains their confidence and encourages their participation.

This form of learning had some interesting beginnings.

HISTORICAL BACKGROUND OF STUDY CIRCLES

Study Circles as a distinct form of education emerged in the United States during the latter half of the 19th century as one element of the Chautauqua Movement, a name derived from Lake Chautauqua, a famous campsite where Sunday School meetings were held. Bishop John H. Vincent created Study Circle groups from the individuals who attended the Chautauqua Literary and Scientific Circle (CISC). Here, people met in small groups to study subjects such as history, art, languages and literature. Many were adults who had never gone to college but who wanted to continue their education. Others among them who had undergraduate degrees wanted to expand their knowledge. CISC members were perhaps first among Americans to practice "lifelong learning." The organization developed printed study circle materials for these courses.

In the early days, bible study for adults became another favorite Study Circle topic, since scriptural classes were then available only in seminaries and ministerial colleges. Soon, social and political topics joined the Social Circle curriculum.

Without a formal "teacher" to lead them, participants in these circles developed a fresh collaborative and interactive approach to adult learning and education different from the traditional classroom format. The Study Circle's interactive model places importance on learning in a social context, not in isolation. Among adults, as experts have discovered, learning is best accomplished by doing and participating, and as a result producing a person who is changed and more experienced.

During the last quarter of the 19th century, Study Circle groups might meet in a church basement, in a back room at a restaurant, in someone's home or anywhere participants could arrange half a dozen chairs in a circle. The Study Circle proved itself as an effective learning tool because, unlike a classroom or lecture format, participants were actively involved in the learning process. They became involved because the subject matter impacted their lives and welfare. Typically, during these sessions bonds of mutual concern began to form between participants, and individuals seemed more personally interested in each other than before. I might mention that I have noticed these positive effects in all of the Study Circles on trauma and emotional recovery I have facilitated.

As the Study Circle in its early days expanded into political topics and public affairs issues, it became a way to educate Americans about political life, democratic methods, community problems and social concerns. After reading a page or two of information about the topic under discussion, Study Circle participants could voice their opinions, share their experiences, present their resources, ask questions, identify problems, and build consensus toward solutions. Most importantly, they learned from one another, they clarified their views, let go of unwarranted assumptions, and discovered they each had something to contribute.

By 1878, 15,000 home study circles were meeting regularly across America using the Chautauqua approach as their form of education and discussion.

At this same time in the United States, there was a great desire for learning among the adult industrialized urban population, many of whom could not afford to leave their jobs to attend college. Organizers of adult civic educational programs offered one solution. They were promoting educational formats involving large public lecture halls and school auditoriums, including the Lyceum Movement, the University Extension Movement, and The Studebaker Public Forum Movement. Such organizers were less interested in small group learning formats where people came together to discuss issues and exchange ideas. Nevertheless, in response to this widespread need and desire for college credits, the Chautauqua Literary and Scientific Circle (CISC) developed a four-year correspondence study based on Home Study Circles.

THE STUDY CIRCLE MOVES TO SWEDEN

Oscar Olson of the Swedish temperance movement visited the United States in 1898 and took the Study Circle idea back to Sweden. Olson became known as the "father of the Study Circle" there, after Study Circles proved to be an effective mechanism for recruiting and educating members of the temperance movement.

During the 19th century Sweden was a bleak nation, its social discontent creating a demand for social change. Popular movements began to emerge, including the temperance movement, the free-church movement, and the blue collar industrial unions. These movements gave the people a framework and a taste for self-government as they fought for basic rights within their society. The leaders of these movements realized that the education of their undereducated members would help bring about a major change in Swedish society. Here's where the Study Circle came in. Not only did it serve as a vehicle for many popular movements to advance their causes and create opportunities for the education of their people, but more importantly it also brought all types of people together. In his book *Study Circles: Coming Together for Personal Growth and Social Change*, Leonard P. Oliver (1987), stated that "following World War II the Study Circle was the most important form of adult civic education in Sweden."[1]

After the war, Sweden's Study Circle activities became even more extensive, involving members of political and religious parties and intramural departments. According to Oliver, "The Swedish government recognized and formalized the practice and organizational structure of Study Circles in 1947 by introducing government grants to subsidize the cost of leader salaries and materials." With the approval of these grants, according to Oliver, came a redefinition of Study Circles as "an informal group which meets for the common pursuit of well-planned studies of a subject or problem area which has previously been decided upon."

In Sweden the use of Study Circles is focused on a simple goal, to promote empowered citizens. For the Swedes, a citizen is empowered by taking part in dialogues about complex issues, where each citizen has a voice and is heard. In Sweden, Study Circles became a way of life, where many adults attended sessions in homes, churches and meeting halls.

STUDY CIRCLES IN THE UNITED STATES SINCE 1970

Almost a century after the Study Circle was born—and almost disappeared— in the United States, it was rediscovered. N. D. Kurland, then Executive Director of Adult Learning Services of the New York State Education Department, traveled to Sweden and Denmark to study the use of Study Circles there. He described his findings in his article "The Scandinavian Study Circle: An Idea for the United States." Based upon his research and with support from the Rockefeller Brothers Fund and the New York State Education Department, he sought to revive the Study Circle concept in the United States. His plan took root in New York where the New York State Study Circle Consortium was established consisting of eight public and private institutions of higher education. In 1980, the consortium ran 400 Study Circle programs across the state in various institutions.

Although this approach has not been followed by other states, the Study Circle movement on its own momentum has grown extensively in recent years. For example, the National Issues Forums supported by the Kettering Foundation has, during the 1980s and 1990s, sponsored up to 5,000 Study Circles a year throughout the United States under the auspices of educational institutions, non-profit organizations and the like.

The Study Circle Resource Center in Pomfret, Connecticut, founded by P. J. Aicher, became the clearinghouse for information about Study Circle activities all over the country and currently provides training materials to groups interested in conducting its programs. The Center also publishes a newsletter with information about the Study Circle community and issues related to Study Circle topics.

In the United States, Study Circle topics are many and varied. Circles have proved to be powerful educational resources not only in civic groups, but also in church societies, other socially concerned groups and in the corporate world. Study Circles are not a replacement, but a versatile enrichment, of our formal educational system. Unlike Sweden, however, the United States federal government is not—as yet—a major supporter of Study Circles.

STUDY CIRCLES USED IN ORGANIZATIONS

Although most Study Circles are community-based, I have found a few reported examples of Study Circles that are corporate-based, which show that the Study Circle is slowly making its way into the organizational life of the United States.

In 1986, for example, the International Union of Bricklayers and Allied Craftsman, a 100,000-member craft union, adopted Study Circles for its member education. In its first year, it trained several Study Circle facilitators, published Study Circle materials and formed 27 Study Circles. The results were overwhelming. Attendance grew and surveys showed strongest interest in studying union issues and members' concerns. About 88% of participants recommended continuation and expansion of the Study Circles. The Bricklayer Study Circle Association now has a full-time staff, a newsletter and strong support from union membership. It has trained over 200 local Study Circle leaders and developed a new Study Circle curriculum that covers topics such as union organizing and health care issues.

At around the same time, DeRidder-Thurston Inc., a manufacturing corporation in Rochester, New York, had concerns with employee motivation and wanted to raise the level of productivity. After examining various techniques available, the staff chose to introduce Study Circles for employees because the concept covered their educational and social needs as well as the employer's needs. The goal was "getting people to work together." Study Circles proved to be very effective in getting people at all levels to talk together which led to more cooperative efforts at work.

My own experience using Study Circles in the federal government proved very successful in educating managers and co-workers about the issues faced by employees returning to work after having a traumatic life experience. After attending the three sessions of this Study Circle, managers reported feeling more confident in approaching such returning employees, having concrete examples of what to do and what not to do, and feeling better equipped than before for interacting with TLE employees. Co-workers learned that each person handles trauma in their own way, how one person's trauma can change the atmosphere and attitudes of the team, and how important it is for the entire team to know how to handle the situation.

STUDY CIRCLES AND GROUP PARTICIPATION

It is difficult to predict which participants will profit most from a Study Circle. Sometimes, the most silent or least obvious contributors may be the ones who are the most self-developing, while the most vocal or active participants may be the ones who, personally, gain the least, even if they seem to have contributed the most.

False assumptions can also inhibit group communication. We can falsely assume we know what others mean when they speak, and others may falsely assume they know what we mean when we speak. In any group, it is likely that each person hears the speaker's message differently and interprets that same message in a different way. After all, each person comes into a group with a personal agenda and for personal reasons. Usually, they are asking themselves, "What do I want to get from this group?" The same is true in a Study Circle, which is why the facilitator's role is so important.

At times individuals may gather in a Study Circle group to discuss very sensitive issues such as race relations and spousal abuse. Peoples' strong feelings on such volatile issues may give rise to unexpected outbursts of emotion. In a conversation with the Study Circle Resource Center in Pomfret, Connecticut, I spoke with Matt Leighninger, its program director, about how Study Circle leaders cope in such situations. He said that the center has no documented research of violent incidents, but suggested that emotional outbursts should be dealt with simply and directly.

Individual feelings and opinions are often expressed during the Study Circle, he said. Therefore, if an outburst occurs, the facilitator ensures that each person in the Study Circle is given a chance to share his point of view, including the person who may have caused the disruption. After all the participants have had an opportunity to talk about what occurred, the Study Circle continues. Mr. Leighninger states this is the process that the Study Circle Resource Center recommends using, and it works.

By ensuring that everyone's views are considered during the discussion, it expands everyone's horizons. In this way, the Study Circle's informal process represents an advance in adult pedagogy because it provides an opportunity for an expression of genuine democracy in local problem solving of community and public issues. The solutions are securely built on the rich experience and combined knowledge of the group. The Study Circle process provides the essential link between learning and life and, in the workplace, between learning and working together.

The Study Circle shows people that they can have voice in their civic or corporate community and the policies that are being made. The Study Circle approach is unique in that it encourages people to formulate their own ideas and share them with others, something seldom done in large meeting halls, public hearings, training sessions or lectures. It is a powerful vehicle for involving people at a fundamental level in the life of their community or organization. It encourages members to become their own experts and to take responsibility for making needed changes.

DRIVEN BY NEED

Since Study Circles are driven primarily by participants' needs, it is appropriate that the content or subject matter should create the need and motivation for the Study Circle. However, in a Study Circle the *process* is just as important as the *content*. Individuals meet and share their experiences about the topic, but the actual learning in a Study Circle occurs collectively when each person hears and relates their personal experience to that of the group.

In each of the Study Circle sessions on workplace trauma that I led, managers and employees practiced active listening skills and received feedback from participants when retelling their trauma stories. One manager shared the story of her trauma when her fiancé was diagnosed with cancer. She was at the time on an upward career path but felt she had to refocus her energies to take care of him. She found her anxiety level was escalating and noticed that she was exhibiting behaviors that she did not view as normal. Because of her fiancé's serious illness she too was traumatized and she constantly talked about what she was experiencing. She stated that talking about it was how she "coped." Participants asked her questions and wanted to learn from her experience. People who had family members with cancer or another terminal illness learned from her ways of coping with it. Participants who did not have such a family member became more sensitive and compassionate toward those who did.

The Study Circle process is not only self-directed and interactive; it is also dynamic and practical. After each Study Circle session, participants begin immediately using what they have learned.

One manager, commenting on the timeliness of the TLE Study Circle for her, stated that within a week of the first session two employees under her care experienced deaths in their family. After listening to the participants exchange ideas in the first Study Circle session, she was able to offer a better level of comfort to these employees upon their return to work. This was something she did not know how to do prior to the Study Circle.

EXPERIENCE-BASED LEARNING

Theorists in adult education usually define mature learning as the *transformation of experience into knowledge, skills and attitudes.* For adults, all learning has an experiential basis. Adults learn best by doing and participating in small groups, thus they are mutually re-creating each other so that each participant is changed and grows wiser. Participants seek to assimilate information in a way that influences their circumstances.

Participants stated that "hearing other people tell their stories," "how they handled their trauma" and "what worked and what did not work" was important for them to hear. Another participant stated that "All of the sessions were helpful, especially the last two, when several people opened up and shared their experiences."

People have an innate desire to learn. Observing the growth of participants' knowledge and of their improving ability to understand and interact with the people around them during a Study Circle session is in itself sufficient payback for their effort. Learning is its own reward.

An interactive learning experience allows for a variety of responses. Growth in knowledge can occur in many different ways, with outcomes personalized to each participant. In a Study Circle, people learn in a participatory environment, continually reflecting on and integrating new information. Participants are enabled to put their lives into perspective and to see their own viewpoints in a wider social context. Adult education is meant to be a living, active process that relates knowledge to action and change, to growth and creativity, to social sensitivity and collective development. The Study Circle process is designed to produce all of these.

THE STUDY CIRCLE:
AN EDUCATIONAL FORMAT
FOR THE ORGANIZATION

Traditionally, in the workplace the three most common educational formats are the lecture, the seminar and the workshop.

The *lecture* is best for communicating and clarifying information, procedures, policies, regulations and the like. It is also used by executives to stir and motivate employees.

The *seminar* format is most often used by corporate leadership to explore and formulate new ideas, policies and procedures—to debate and discuss them before implementing them.

The *workshop* is used primarily for training people in various skills; it is a very practical educational model with developing a very specific performance skill in the learners as its main purpose. It is usually run by trainers who are experts in that skill.

What has been missing in the workplace is *an educational process for dealing with topics that need to be learned attitudinally,* that is, topics that are aimed at transforming not only knowledge and behavior but also attitudes and emotions. In dealing with the re-entry of a TLE employee, it is not enough to present the kinds of knowledge and information given in a lecture, nor is it enough to include a set of behavioral skills that one might learn in a workshop. The "missing" educational format needs also to provide ways to educate attitudes and emotions as well. The Study Circle is able to provide this missing dimension of the traditional learning process in the workplace. The personal sharing in the Study Circle by participants who had experienced a traumatic life event or had managed a returning TLE employee provided the context for the needed attitudinal and emotional learning to take place in a practical and realistic way.

For example, consider Gwen's story. If she was absent from your office and came back to work a week after her traumatic life experience, would you know how to deal with her—what to say and what not to say, what to do and what not to do—if you were her manager or one of her co-workers? Here's her story.

Gwen, who worked as one of a large group of claims processors for a major health insurance company, went home as usual after work last Tuesday. She got off her bus and stopped at the local market for a few things she needed for dinner that evening. When she opened the door of the apartment, some things just didn't look right but it wasn't enough to bother her. Her eight-year-old daughter was watching television.

"Daddy left an envelope for you on the kitchen table," the girl said.

Gwen walked into the kitchen, unsealed the envelope, read the note and stood there in shock. In the note, George, her husband of ten years, announced that he had taken his things and had left to start a new life. "I'm not ever coming back," was the last line of the note.

As she walked around in a daze, Gwen realized the house had looked unusual because George had removed various things, including the stereo and the CD collection that went with it, all his sports equipment, his clothing, and his laptop computer. When she saw the empty garage, she realized George had also taken the family car. The next morning Gwen would discover he had also wiped clean both their checking account and their savings account.

"Did daddy say where he was going?" Gwen asked her daughter.

"I didn't see him at all," she replied. "He must have left before I got home."

"How did you know about the note he left for me?" she asked.

"I saw it when I was getting milk and cookies," said her daughter.

Gwen realized her daughter was totally unaware that her father had abandoned both of them.

Next morning, Gwen telephoned her manager at work and said she would be taking a few days of personal leave.

"Sure, Gwen," the manager said. "We'll cover for you. But are you all right? I hope nothing is wrong with you or your family?"

"It's nothing. I just need a few days to straighten out some things here," she answered.

Gwen wasn't about to tell him that her husband had just left them without any warning or money, and that he had probably run off with his pretty secretary, (a supposition that later turned out to be true). It was painfully embarrassing to have to shift in a moment from being a contented wife and mother to being someone your husband would drop, disown, steal from, and replace with a younger more attractive model. "I'm a failure as a wife," she said to herself.

Eventually, people at work will have to learn about this, she thought, but not yet. "How can I ever face the people I work with?" she said aloud, as she pictured people looking up from their desks at her the day she walked into work for the first time. She felt ashamed just thinking about it.

Undoubtedly, her manager, when he discovers Gwen's situation and predicament, will refer her to human resources for counseling and legal assistance. But, how should her manager and co-workers treat her? As if all her troubles were none of their business? As if nothing bad had ever happened? As if everything was back to normal now? Or should they pity her behind her back?

Such treatment could easily reinforce her shame and embarrassment, convince her that she had been a bad wife and mother, and prove that she was not someone worth showing compassion toward. None of this would help Gwen's recovery, rebuild her spirit of work, and get her back feeling a part of the team.

Moreover, there is no simple formula on what to say or do in dealing in a caring manner with a returning TLE employee like Gwen. Each trauma survivor is a unique personality with different needs and expectations. For Gwen, even though in the long—and short—run resolving her financial situation would be most crucial, her main concern was her shame and embarrassment returning to the workplace.

Only in hearing a number of trauma stories and talking them over, as would happen in a Study Circle, would the participants come to develop a sense of or attitude toward the emotional recovery process for survivors like Gwen.

If the Study Circle process were working well, after hearing her story, each participant would be asking himself or herself, "How can I help *put out a welcome mat* for Gwen? How can I *lend a listening ear* to let her tell her story to me if she wants to? How can I *offer a helping hand* to help her reconnect with Gwen so that she really feels a valuable part of our team again?" And each one would be sharing his or her thoughts and ideas with the other participants.

THE STUDY CIRCLE'S DEMOCRATIC SPIRIT

Another educational dynamic characteristic of the Study Circle process is its "democratic" spirit. When properly conducted, a Study Circle makes every participant equal and values everyone's contribution. This democratic spirit in the TLE Study Circle allows managers and employees to share their experiences and discuss the topic as equals. A rather revolutionary event in corporate life!

Whereas the task of helping the successful re-entry of a TLE employee would normally fall to a counselor or therapist, the Study Circle format allows participants, not to assume the work of the therapist, but to learn to support and promote that work in ways appropriate to managers and co-workers.

An adequate understanding of this work of support that can be provided by managers and co-workers could not have happened in a traditional lecture or workshop, but only in a holistic learning format where personal experience and empathy along with the expression of attitudes, emotions and values are included. The Study Circle format puts these experiential and emotional factors at the center of its learning process.

The Study Circle as an educational format can also prove useful with a topic around which organizational policies and procedures have *not yet* been formulated and institutionalized. Treatment of the returning TLE employee by managers and co-workers is one such focus. Because such treatment requires a major involvement with empathy, attitudes and emotional sensitivity, it is not an appropriate topic for legislation by executives or presentation in a seminar. The Study Circle format invites participants to share their personal views around such topics, and it views this personal experience as important data in helping shape procedures and policies. In summary, the Study Circle process, as an adult learning format, can fill a missing dimension among the educational tools currently used in the organizational workplace.

THE STUDY CIRCLE: A PSYCHOLOGICAL PROCESS

Some may object to the claim that the Study Circle is an educational process, not primarily a psychological one. They may assert that the participants use the sessions as a psychological process, no matter what anyone may claim. "What you're promoting with a Study Circle," is nothing more than group therapy."

I assure you that the Study Circle is not a group therapy session. Although the two processes have some elements in common—both call for trust, group cohesion and a willingness to share personal experiences—there are many elements that differentiate them. Each Study Circle has its own specific topic, e.g., "the returning TLE employee," while the topic of group therapy is always the same—*the psychological health of the individual group members.* In a Study Circle, specific conceptual material is discussed, and the facilitator has a list of questions about the topic that help define the sequence of the process. Thus, each Study Circle on the returning TLE will follow the same sequence, and in the end each Study Circle group will have covered the same material. None of these elements is true of therapy groups.

Some have claimed that Study Circles are merely another name for "rap groups." Although it is not a therapeutic intervention, the Study Circle has elements similar to the rap group process, which is primarily therapeutic. Rap groups were introduced in 1970 by Jay Lifton and Chaim Shatan, psychiatrists who invited Viet Nam veterans to retell their stories of war trauma to each other. Veterans who were "hurting" felt comfortable in this setting as it provided a safe context in which to reconstruct their trauma story outside of a traditional psychiatric setting. It was here in these rap groups that psychological trauma was first identified by the psychiatric professionals as a "real diagnosis," and eventually PTSD (Post-traumatic Stress Disorder) was recognized formally in its diagnostic manuals by the American Psychological Association.

The big distinction between the rap group and a Study Circle is that the group members in a rap group are trying to heal themselves. In contrast, the people in a TLE Study Circle are not trying to heal themselves but rather to understand the emotional process of recovery going on in their fellow employees returning to the workplace after a traumatic life experience.

It might be clarifying to make a few additional distinctions. First, although the Study Circle *topic* might be concerned with a psychological process, e.g., the psychological recovery of the TLE employee, such a topic may still be treated educationally, for example, as having concepts and procedures to be identified, defined and understood, that is, learned. Thus, participants learned the concept of the "putting out a welcome mat" and the procedures for evoking "lending a listening ear."

Secondly, since the Study Circle process involves the physical, mental, emotional and social dimensions of all participants, it is not surprising that the participants notice emotional and attitudinal changes happening in themselves, as well as conceptual and behavioral ones. Good education always changes the whole person, not just the intellect. Moreover, workplace participants are more likely to notice the psychological dynamics happening in a Study Circle, since in most other forms of workplace education such as lectures, seminars and training workshops, psychological dynamics play a much less significant part.

Finally, it is not surprising that Study Circle participants are very aware of the interplay of emotions and attitudes that happen during the sessions. This is precisely because the topic of a Study Circle is one in which participants are personally and emotionally involved. It is precisely because the participants are so involved that the Study Circle process is as effective as an educational format. It allows people who have strong feelings about a certain topic to meet together in a structured learning process that encourages everyone to share their own personal experiences, not merely "thoughts," about the topic.

The Study Circle format ensures that this is done in ways that end up, not in debate and competition, but in learning from each other.

COGNITIVE LEARNING

The Study Circle's cognitive component helps the participants learn new responses from each other. They are able to develop and apply new behaviors related to what they learn. In a Study Circle I conducted, one participant stated that it was important for the managers to show "empathy" towards the returning TLE employee. Participants then engaged in an intellectual discussion about the meaning of "empathy" and addressed their questions to each other on how a person shows empathy. This issue created an on-going dialogue throughout the three Study Circle sessions.

Another subject that provoked cognitive discussion among the managers was "productivity versus compassion." Some managers were concerned with recent downsizing within their organizations and the loss of resources. Conflict and ambivalence surfaced among them when they started to differentiate between being concerned with "the bottom line" and showing "compassion" to the returning TLE employee.

The handouts provided by the researcher prior to each Study Circle Session also served as a cognitive learning resource to the participants. Both managers and employees referred to the helpfulness of these handouts that guided them through each session.

The Study Circle educational model presented the participants with an opportunity to think, feel and act differently about a new topic.

AFFECTIVE LEARNING

In a Study Circle, participants get in touch with their attitudes, feelings and preferences regarding returning TLE employees. This occurs through the dialogue, sharing, interaction and networking that is typically created among the participants. The Study Circle facilitator allows the dialogue to emerge by letting participants ask each other questions and inquiring about the extent of their own traumas.

In one session, I recall when managers were discussing performance and behavioral problems of TLE employees, they felt that these problems could become serious if the persons were not supported in the workplace. After a session, it is not unusual that a few in the group remain in the room to keep talking about how to handle a returning TLE employee.

One manager who had himself returned to work after a TLE expressed the importance of being hugged by a few people on his return and being made to feel welcomed back. He specifically mentioned the words "dialogue," "sharing feelings," "physical associations" and stated that all of these expressions of care meant a lot to him and felt it would mean a lot to another person in the same situation.

Affective learning is accomplished in the Study Circle sessions through interaction and discussion that allows managers and employees to become aware of each other's perceptions and feelings.

Now, the question is: How do we set up an on-site Study Circle for managers and co-workers to help them understand traumatic life experiences and understand the emotional recovery process of the returning TLE employee.

NOTE

1. *Study Circles: Coming Together for Personal Growth and Social Change.* (Washington, D.C., Seven Locks Press, 1987) p. 5.

Chapter Nine

How Does an Organization Set Up a Study Circle?

INTRODUCTION

This chapter offers suggestions for selecting participants, procedures for conducting the Study Circle, and the roles of participant and facilitator.

As indicated earlier, Dr. Judith Lewis Herman (1992) in her book *Trauma and Recovery* described three stages that are required for the successful recovery and re-entry of the traumatized person into normal life. A major part of normal life is lived out in the workplace. Accordingly, these three stages were selected as the themes underlying the three Study Circle sessions.

Session 1. Putting out a welcome mat for the returning TLE employee
Session 2. Lending a listening ear for the person to tell their trauma experience
Session 3. Offering a helping hand to reconnecting the TLE employee to the work community

The *first session* in the Study Circle focuses on what *putting out a welcome mat* may mean to the survivor and how management can establish a safe haven for the returning TLE employee. A safe haven is a place where someone can go for comfort in trying to deal with their emotional pain. The welcome mat concept extends to a person's home and work environment and, in its broadest meaning, includes a safe living situation, financial security, mobility and a plan for self-protection. It may also include concern for the survivor's body and related basic health needs, sleep, eating and exercise. Providing a safe place usually also encompasses a social support system that needs to be established by the survivors—people who will not tease, taunt, threaten, shame, or pressure them or pry into painful emotions and memories.

Putting out a welcome mat is important because when a trauma occurs, survivors are likely to feel powerless and robbed of control over themselves. They may feel unsafe in relation to other people, especially if they are returning to work after a long absence. "Is my job still mine?" "Has someone else been doing it better in my absence?" "Will my co-workers welcome me back?" "Will they still like me?" These and many other questions go through their minds. Because of the time taken away from work by the trauma experience, TLE employees may not know if and when they will get paid and if they can have additional time off if they need it. For them, these are issues of safety and security.

Consider the case of Gwen being abandoned by her husband, the story I told in the previous chapter. If she worked in your office, how would you begin to create a safe haven for her? How would you go about finding out what was worrying her, what questions she was asking herself about the people in her office and how they would treat her on her return?

The *second session* discusses the usefulness of having the TLE employee reveal his trauma story and the pain associated around the experience he felt to people in the workplace. And so it is important that fellow employees *lend a listening ear* to the returning person. Research has shown that storytelling is particularly important to a TLE employee when he or she returns to work. But only when and if the person is ready and willing to share their experience. Reconstructing the traumatic experience with colleagues is likely to be beneficial in the emotional recovery process, if it is done with care and concern. The discussion within the second Study Circle session focuses on whether, how and when the trauma story can be reconstructed by the TLE employees upon returning to the workplace, and how managers and co-workers might best help allow it to happen. Could you guess a few reasons why Gwen would not want to elaborate to her colleagues when she returned to work? Do you think Gwen would be ready to relate her whole story to you her first day back to work?

The theme of the Study Circle's *third session* is all about reconnecting the TLE employee to the work community. This theme is important because returning TLE employees may need to reclaim their "lost world," re-establish relationships with managers and co-workers, and build a new workplace life. Here's where fellow employees can *offer a helping hand* to the returning person. The manager also plays a key role. In this session, the discussion usually revolves around the manager's role and how the manager can assist TLE employees reconnect with their co-workers, a bond which survivors often feel they may have lost because of the trauma.

Gwen sees herself now as a very different person from the one she was who left work so happily last Tuesday. If you were her manager or a fellow employee reconnecting with her, should you try to reconnect with the old Gwen or the "different" Gwen?

SELECTING PARTICIPANTS

Participants in any TLE Study Circle should include both managers and employees. The managers observe the employees in this sharing dialogue, and employees observe the managers. If every participant hasn't had a personal traumatic life experience (TLE), they all know of others who have. If they personally don't know what it is like to re-enter the workplace after having experienced a trauma, they have probably heard comments from those who have been through the process. When there is a mix of employees and managers, all gain awareness from each other on how to address the TLE employee re-entering the workplace.

I suggest that the organization preparing to conduct this Study Circle canvass for volunteers to participate. A Study Circle's success depends on participants who are very interested and invested in the topic and *want* to participate.

I also suggest an invitation along with a confidential agreement be given to each participant before the first session. (See samples at end of chapter.) The invitation confirms the participant's role in the Study Circle and the confidential agreement protects any participant disclosing to others information of a personal nature heard during the Study Circle sessions. Remind participants of the time and place of each session with a telephone call or an email message.

A good mix of volunteers for a Study Circle on returning TLE employees would include people from the four following groups:

1. Managers who have supervised a returning TLE employee.
2. Managers who have not supervised a returning TLE employee.
3. Managers who have/and have not had a personal traumatic life experience (TLE).
4. Employees who have themselves experienced a TLE.

In recruiting participants for the Study Circle, in addition to a mix of labor and management, a mix of personalities is preferred. For example, if all participants in one group are accountants the session may not result in a rich dialogue with diverse opinions because of the composition of the group. On the other hand, I have never facilitated a group that did not result in a rich dialogue, no matter what the mix of participants.

A few—very few, in my experience—participants may refuse to become involved in the Study Circle process. They may be reticent to dialogue or share their thoughts with the group. For some of these, all they need is a word of encouragement and to be directly invited to share. If a simple direct invitation doesn't work, I have found that if I make the effort to speak with such a person in private, I can usually encourage them to be more forthcoming in the next session.

In your organization, it may be a Human Resources person who does the interviews, schedules the sessions, and acts as facilitator. Or it may be someone else. Interviews are not strictly necessary, as long as the participants are interested and have an investment in the topic.

INTERVIEWS

When I first began facilitating this TLE Study Circle in my department in the federal government, I found it very useful to conduct individual Pre-Study Circle interviews privately with members of each group, for several reasons. I used these interviews to provide participants with an overview of the scope and purpose of the Study Circle, and to introduce the three Study Circle themes, obtain some background information about them to familiarize myself with them, and learn about their own trauma stories.

In some very few cases, for example, with people who were too close to their trauma and some who were still in shock, I discouraged them from attending. For example, I would discourage someone like Gwen from attending during the first few weeks after her return to work, since her traumatic experience may be still too raw and painful for her to benefit from it. But I would encourage her manager and co-workers to attend. Actually, I would wish they had participated in a TLE Study Circle *before* Gwen had her TLE.

During these interviews I encourage people to share their stories in one or other of the Study Circle sessions, and even specifically request of them, "Be sure to include this or that part of your story when you tell us about it." The questions I ask the participants during the interview provide an opportunity for me to observe their reactions to the topic. The pre-Study Circle interview also gives participants a chance to ask me questions and think, prior to meeting, about the Study Circle and what will be discussed.

At the end of this chapter, I include a list of questions I use in conducting these interviews. I still conduct individual interviews for Study Circle group members whenever possible.

Because many of my colleagues were aware of this project when I first started it, and the need to recruit participants for my pilot studies, people in different divisions of the agency made referrals. From among these, I selected individuals based upon participant interest in the topic and whether they were willing to sign on for the Study Circle, making a personal commitment of time and energy. Ultimately, all participants were selected on a volunteer basis. My pilot groups included Caucasian, Afro-American, American Indian and Hispanic participants.

In each group, these participants fell into four categories: (1) senior level managers who had not had a traumatic life experience nor supervised any returning TLE employees; (2) senior level managers who had had a traumatic experience and had supervised returning TLE employees; (3) senior level managers who had not had a traumatic experience but who had supervised at least one returning TLE employee; (4) TLE employees who had made a successful re-entry to their workplace environment.

It is suggested, but not required, that the facilitator of the Study Circle interview all named participants prior to the Study Circle sessions. Usually interviewing is necessary in an organization where recently there has been intense trauma elsewhere in the country, such as the Oklahoma Bombing, Post Office shootings or terrorist attacks. After such events, anxiety is high everywhere and managers and employees may feel ambivalent about return-ing to work, even half a continent away from the traumatic event. Pre-session interviews, especially at these times, can help participants, become comfort-able with the facilitator and the ambiance of the proposed Study Circle.

In general, the interview makes the facilitator aware of the kinds of traumas participants have experienced and their comfort level in talking about them. If an organization chooses not to do the pre-Study Circle interviews, the Study Circle will still be effective.

PRELIMINARY PROCEDURES AND LOGISTICS

Prior to beginning the Study Circle, participants should be given printed ma-terials to read—a page or two—explaining the Study Circle process and the roles of participants and facilitator.

Before each session participants should also receive handout materials about the topic prior to theme of each session. These handouts serve as refer-ence for definitions of terms and questions for discussion. Participants ap-preciate having these handouts at least a few days before the session so they can mull over the questions in the meantime.

Each Study Circle consists of three two-hour sessions. In my pilot groups, each session ran across the lunch hour, from 11:30 a.m. to 1:30 p.m. This proved to be an excellent time, convenient for both senior managers and other employees. In most cases, in a workplace setting a brown bag lunch is appropriate. My office provided a boxed lunch for each participant. Sharing lunch together at 11:30 served as a social warm-up for everyone and, in its own way, provided an incentive for the participants to share their experiences in the group. In most cases, people were ready and eager to begin the session even before they had finished eating.

The sessions were held in an available seminar room in our building, which offered easy access to all participants, few distractions and lack of noise. I found it helpful to schedule Study Circles sessions one week apart to give participants an opportunity to digest and, if possible, practice what they learned.

In general, sessions should be held in the workplace building, perhaps in a large conference room with ample space for individuals to move around in comfort. For this Study Circle, the maximum group size is fifteen individuals; the minimum is eight or ten. This guarantees rich and varied input. Ask participants to sit in a circle so that each person can see the faces of all others.

GETTING STARTED

To get the discussion started, I usually begin by posing probing questions to the participants and I continue this approach throughout the session. This helps keep the discussion focused on the session's theme. As you watch a group deal with a question, the power of the Study Circle's collaborative learning environment quickly becomes clear. The discussion is driven primarily by the participants' needs and interests. As participants share their experiences, learning occurs. You can see the lights going on in peoples' minds. Each person hears the experiences of other group members and relates it to their personal situation.

In the first session of one Study Circle I led, I told Gwen's story and asked, if Gwen had been a co-worker of theirs, how they would have put out a welcome mat for her. One participant said that when we had been discussing the *concept* of the welcome mat, he thought it would be very easy to design a generic welcome mat package *in the workplace* for any returning TLE employee, and there would be no need for a Study Circle on the that idea. But after he heard Gwen's story, he realized such a generic package wouldn't be so easy to design, as she had lots of emotional assumptions going on inside her that her co-workers couldn't know about and might never know about until she told them. And since she was probably not ready to tell them what she was thinking and feeling about herself, her fellow employees would be hard pressed to come up with sure-fire suggestions for creating a safe haven.

As soon as this man stopped talking, people began realizing how each returning TLE employee has a unique personality so there could be no set formula for creating a welcoming ceremony that would work for everyone. It had to be designed to fit their personality.

And someone added, "But Gwen had really changed her self-image between the time she left work the previous Tuesday and the day she returned the following week. She went home on Tuesday feeling like a happy and successful wife and she returned, though we didn't know it at the time, like a sad failure of a wife. So, which Gwen are we supposed to put out the welcome mat for?"

And would the unique safe haven we created for Gwen also work for the woman who returns to work after being raped or robbed on the street or whose car is hijacked? Or will it work for the employee whose spouse has a heart attack? Or for an employee diagnosed with a terminal illness? Or one whose mother suddenly dies?

The problem of employees returning to the workplace after a traumatic life experience has become increasingly urgent both to managers and co-workers, requiring that they possess both a theoretical and practical grasp of the issue. Theoretically, the Study Circle introduces participants to the concepts of understanding the emotional recovery of trauma and the process that the re-entry employee will be going through. Practically, it teaches them how to talk and interact with TLE employees in such a way that the healing process is helped, not hindered.

OVERVIEW OF A FIRST SESSION

1. Invite introductions. I begin the Study Circle's first session by having all the participants sit around a table or in a circle and introduce themselves. It's important to ask each participant to identify the specific division or branch that they are working in. This helps identify the organizational setting.

2. Explain ground rules. I then discuss the facilitator's role and the importance of keeping the Study Circle discussion focused. I explain to the group not to be afraid of conflict issues that may come to the surface, and I encourage participants to engage in active dialogue. I also remind them of confidentiality as a protection for everyone concerned.

3. Discuss topic. I emphasize to the group the fact of their commitment to the topic being discussed and their desire to learn more about it. If the participants have strong feelings about the topic, this is generally good because it increases participation. I find it helpful to have a list of questions for discussion specific to each session. This helps me keep the discussion moving and focused. In general, I found individuals much more verbal and open to sharing during the Study Circle sessions than they were in the interview.

4. Summarize points. I encourage participants to engage one another, to share their points of view and probe for more answers when an explanation may not seem clear. I watch for patterns of insight or key points that may occur during the group discussion and summarize those for the participants, either when they are happening or near the end of the session.

5. Evaluate the session. Before we leave the room, I like to talk to the group about the learning process, find out what they liked and did not like during the session, and how the process could be improved. I learned that, before the group disperses, I need to remind the individuals about the reading the handout and mulling over the discussion questions before the next Study Circle session.

THE FACILITATOR ROLE

The facilitator does not have to possess expert knowledge on the topic of the Study Circle; however he must be familiar enough with the subject matter to guide the participants through each session. If an organization chooses to have the facilitator conduct pre-Study Circle interviews, the facilitator will also gain first-hand knowledge of each individual's trauma experience. If interviews are not conducted, the Study Circle can move along as planned. The facilitator may need to be more observant, sensitive and creative. That's all.

There are a few points important for a facilitator to remember when guiding a session.

1. Understand group process. Remember that your group will be composed of many different personalities who may share different values. Usually, each group forms its own group culture and develops its own timing and style for sharing thoughts, feelings and experiences with each other. It's important to keep the group focused on the content of the subject matter. As a facilitator, you will learn that natural "moments of silence" at times may be good for the group, allowing them to process their thoughts, questions and ideas.

2. Set a participative tone. As participants enter the meeting room, be sure to welcome each one and personally encourage them to participate. If this Study Circle is one where a sensitive subject will be addressed, the facilitator should remember to allow participants to be themselves, and assure them that their experiences will add to the group dialogue.

3. Work with Content. It's important for the facilitator to focus on the topic and foster a lively exchange between members of the group. Asking probing questions and referring to specific discussion questions is the best way of getting others to participate and staying focused.

4. Discuss questions. Well-focused discussion questions handed out before each session can reduce pressure on the facilitator immensely. If such questions are printed in the session handout, they serve as a reference both for the participants and the facilitator.

5. Close the discussion. When the topic has been discussed sufficiently, the facilitator takes the initiative to ask the group whether anything has been missed during the group exchange.

6. Summarize the session. To remind participants of what they have learned during this session, the facilitator might ask questions like:

  a. What thoughts are you leaving this Study Circle with today?
  b. When you return to the workplace, will you feel more confident in dealing with a returning TLE? Why?
  c. Will you be able to share some of your concerns with others?
  d. What did you learn today that you can use practically?

FACILITATORS SHARING THEIR OWN TRAUMA STORIES

A facilitator can be especially effective if he or she personally had a traumatic life experience or supervised an individual who re-entered the workplace after having one. Although prior personal experience of a trauma is not required, the facilitator's sensitivity and ability to share such a personal experience in the group sets a tone of sharing. It presents an invitation and gives permission for others to share their stories. For example, in the Study Circle's second session I often begin by sharing my trauma story with the group—the death of my father. I would tell them not merely the facts surrounding his death, but also what went on inside me when it happened. I would tell them that my father had been a friend and mentor to me all through my career, someone I could always lean on and count on. When he died, it felt like I had lost one of my arms. I described how I felt off balance; as though I would have to relearn how to stand up straight and how to do things I was used to doing but now with one arm missing. "In a way," I would explain, "I had to reorient my whole life." Telling your story models for participants how they might begin to tell of their own traumatic life experiences.

Soon afterwards, other members begin to share their own stories and a new level of interaction and trust emerges. As a facilitator, telling your personal story enables other participants to feel a level of comfort with you. It also sets the tone for further openness, encouraging other participants to retell their trauma experiences.

In a Study Circle the role of the facilitator is unique and should not be confused with leaders in other types of group work. For example, often a Study Circle facilitator is inaccurately described as a mediator. At the outset, the two facilitating roles may seem similar, but their objectives are totally different. In mediation, parties in disagreement are brought together to negotiate a settlement and resolve a conflict. This is not so in a Study Circle. There is no disagreement to be negotiated. People are coming together to learn from each other. The main task for the facilitator in a Study Circle is to assist and improve the group process and help people develop more effective interpersonal behavior as this learning happens.

SAMPLE MATERIAL FOR FACILITATORS

Letter of Invitation for Participants

Dear Participant,

I would like to invite you to participate in a Study Circle titled "Helping Managers and Co-Workers Deal with an Employee Returning to the Workplace After a Traumatic Life Experience (TLE)."

I have long been professionally interested in creating positive work environments. Organizations today are continually faced with the issue of effectively assimilating TLE employees who are returning to their jobs. Dealing with such individuals poses a unique dilemma to organizations and, in particular, to managers and co-workers who have the responsibility of assisting such returning survivors to make the transition as smoothly, effectively and quickly as possible. Many managers and co-workers have little or no idea how best to do this, mostly because they do not understand the stages of emotional recovery that a traumatized person will normally go through. This Study Circle is designed to fill that gap.

A Study Circle is a specially designed form of adult education that has been used successfully for over 100 years. It is especially effective in dealing with sensitive issues of interest to participants. During Study Circle sessions complex issues are broken down into manageable discussion points and controversial topics are discussed in depth.

In this Study Circle, about 8 – 12 people will meet for three sessions. Each session will last for no more than two hours with a mix of managers and employees in the group. I will discuss with each participant the scheduling of the Study Circle sessions. It is important that you participate in all three sessions. The proposed schedule is:

Session	Theme	Date	Time	Location
1.	Putting out a Welcome Mat			
2.	Lending a Listening Ear			
3.	Offering a Helping Hand			

One of the best aspects of Study Circles is that expertise on the topic under discussion is not necessary. Rather, Study Circles are a learning format through which people like you and I can bring the experience of ordinary people to bear on important workplace issues. All you need is a willingness to participate in the discussions and to really want to hear what others have to say. I can promise you the discussions will be spirited, cordial, and informative and—best of all—fun!

I will contact you in a few days to discuss any questions you may have and deliver materials for our first Study Circle session. If you have any questions, please call me.

Sincerely,

Confidentiality Agreement

I, *(Participant)*, as a condition of participating in the Study Circle sessions for "Helping Managers and Co-Workers Deal with an Employee Returning to the Workplace After a Traumatic Life Experience (TLE)," being facilitated by *(Your Name)* at *(Location)* on *(Dates)* hereby agree that I will not, directly or indirectly, divulge or otherwise make known to any person or entity any personal information of any type disclosed by other participants during the course of the said Study Circle.

I understand that any information disclosed by participants in the Study Circle sessions is personal and confidential in nature, and that any information that I may provide during the course of the Study Circle will be treated as such by all other participants each of whom will be required to sign a Confidentiality Statement identical to this one as a condition of their participation in the Study Circle sessions.

Facilitator's Signature   *Participant's Signature*

Date   *Date*

PRE-STUDY CIRCLE INTERVIEW QUESTIONS

Some of these questions may be used by the facilitator prior to the Study Circle sessions to interview managers and employees. Let the organization and the facilitator discern whether pre-Study Circle interviews should be carried out.

The following questions are suggested to explore a participant's experience and understanding of traumatic life experiences and their effects in the workplace. These are questions I generally ask of participants during interviews prior to the first Study Circle session:

1. Did you ever have a personal experience with trauma? If so, how did you handle it? What was your experience in returning to work afterward?
2. Did you ever have a co-worker who experienced a trauma and returned to the workplace? What did you say to that person up their return? How did you treat that person?

3. If an employee were returning to the workplace today after having experienced a trauma, how would you behave toward that person? Have your ideas about treating such a person changed over time?

4. Have you ever observed an employee talking with a co-worker and sharing their trauma story upon their return to the workplace?

5. Would you normally ask the returning employee to tell of their experience or share their story upon returning to the workplace?

6. How comfortable do you feel approaching or talking to a person who has just returned to work after having experienced a trauma?

7. Do you know what things to say to a returning TLE employee that will help them feel welcome when they return to work?

8. How would you go about assisting the returning TLE employee to participate in office activities?

9. How would you respond to a TLE employee who refuses to work and begins to have emotional outbursts?

10. Do you think gender plays a role in dealing with a returning TLE employee? Do women behave differently from men when they return to the workplace?

Manager only questions:

1. Did you ever supervise a person who returned to the workplace after having experienced a trauma? (If so, how did you handle it?)

2. What approach would you use if you had to communicate your expectations to a person on their first day back to work after having experienced a trauma?

3. How would you go about explaining to your staff the importance of greeting and talking with the person who is returning to the workplace after their trauma.

4. What would you do if you had to set limits with a returning TLE employee when he returns to work, e.g., if the person started coming to work consistently late?

5. How would you state work assignments and expectations of productivity to the returning TLE employee?

Chapter Ten

Putting Out a Welcome Mat:
The First Study Circle

INTERACTIVE LEARNING

In working with and training adults over the past twenty years, I have concluded, with many practitioners of adult education, that adults learn best through interactive forms of education. That is, when you bring individuals together to discuss a sensitive topic which they all share and about which they have strong feelings, it proves to be a powerful educational force. Because of the Study Circle's interactive nature, participants during the sessions discover themselves as part of a new and intimate group culture that they themselves create. Because each Study Circle finds its own pace and rhythm, it's hard to predict what will happen when a diverse group of people join together to discuss an emotionally charged topic. However, you can be sure it will be interesting, lively and transforming. And, as evidenced from the continuous interactive involvement of all the participants, the process consistently proves very beneficial.

In each of the three Study Circle sessions, participants explore what is needed in an organization so managers and employees can help understand the emotional recovery process in a returning TLE employee. The first session focuses on *putting out a welcome mat* for the returning TLE employee; the second centers around *lending a listening ear* to understanding how retelling the trauma experience story can influence emotional recovery; and in the third participants *offering a helping hand* to seek to find ways help the TLE employee reconnect to the workplace.

GETTING STARTED

Before each session, each participant is given a handout describing the theme to be discussed during the Study Circle session plus some questions to

96

stimulate dialogue. For example, for the "welcome mat" session, participants mulled over questions like the following:

a. *What would it take to put out a welcome mat in your workplace environ-ment for a returning TLE employee?*
b. *What would it look like and feel like if your workplace was emotionally "unsafe" for a returning TLE employee?*
c. *In your workplace, what are some of the current typical reactions of people to returning TLE employees?*
d. *What kinds of questions might you ask the returning TLE employee to find out what would make them feel personally welcome?*

Usually when TLE employees return to the workplace, they are anxious and ambivalent about how they will be seen and treated by their co-workers, especially if their traumatic experience has kept them from work for an ex-tended period of time. Consequently, they may be hesitant about immediately socializing with fellow employees and may feel they don't quite belong to the organization yet.

Outside work, they may be seeing a social worker or therapist for grief work or depression, and may be taking medication that affects their ability to focus. Because of this, they may act strangely or impetuously on the job. They may feel emotionally unsafe or embarrassed among their co-workers, as they tend not to have their customary control over their emotions and reac-tions.

Some returning TLE employees are not sure how to behave in workplace situations where previously they had acted with confidence. Someone else has obviously been doing their job while they were home or hospitalized, and they wonder if the person who temporarily replaced them will be doing so permanently.

Because they probably also have difficulty sleeping at night and concen-trating during the day, this may manifest itself at work as an inability to complete tasks they could easily do before the traumatic experience. After a trauma, some may want to go into seclusion and hide from others. Their old reality seems broken and nothing feels solid or certain anymore.

Managers and co-workers are often confused and uncomfortable in relating to a TLE employee when he or she first returns to work.

WHAT DOES IT MEAN TO PUT OUT A WELCOME MAT?

As participants in the first session discuss feelings of security with the return-ing TLE employees, the question naturally arises about the types of welcome mats a traumatized person might need. The obvious way to begin is to ask

TLE survivors in the group what their managers and co-workers could have done to make the workplace a safe haven to come back to after their traumatic life experience.

Each group will probably put a different meaning on a "welcome mat" that provides safety and security. One group might list things like financial assistance and/or support from the organization, time off that may be needed for psychological readjustment, flexibility with work assignments, empathy and trust.

Another group, taking a different approach, might want to identify the natural welcoming gestures that already exist in organizations, such as ongoing friendships at the workplace, the natural and spontaneous bonding that occurs between colleagues, managers and supervisors.

A third group, feeling that the task of creating a safe haven falls primarily upon managers, might list their advice to the manager saying what he should do upon the TLE employee's return. This is a common turn for Study Circle groups in the first session, especially because mangers do not always know what to do or say, and enough of them are willing to admit it. Here is a short summary of advice one group gave managers:

a. Let the TLE employee set the pace. Follow the flow of the employee.
b. Express empathy toward the returning TLE employee.
c. Remember that when individuals return to the workplace they want normalcy as much as you do, but they realize it won't happen immediately and certainly not without your help.

Many managers may find it difficult to follow the employee, but those who are trauma survivors agree the company would have gotten more from them if managers had been able to take the lead from the survivor.

As for "expressing empathy," the second recommendation, it is much easier said than done. Few of us are in the habit of expressing empathy because it begins with a special kind of empathic listening, according to Stephen J. Covey (1989) in his book *The Seven Habits of Highly Effective People*. He says that empathic listening requires that, in our minds, we move into the frame of reference of the other person and listen as if we were inside them, feeling what they feel and seeing the world as they see it.

Instead, Covey says, when we hear others talking, we usually remain in our own frame of reference. When in that self-focused attitude, we mostly *don't listen at all*. At this level, as the other person speaks, we aren't listening to them, but rather thinking of what we will say next.

Sometimes, we go one step further beyond not-listening and *listen selectively*. We hear what we want to hear, what will promote what we want to say or get done, and disregard the rest of what the other person says.

A very few go the second step and *listen attentively*, but like an opponent in a debate everything we hear gets processed through our own personal agenda. We look for slip-ups, loopholes, errors, incorrect facts in what the other person says—whatever will help us win the debate.

Empathic listening is not a skill someone learns by merely wishing for it. It takes practice built upon a strong compassion for others.

In one discussion about expressing empathy to the returning TLE employee, the managers pointed out that, though empathic listening sounds like a great approach, they face a very complex issue because, besides going through an emotional recovery process, survivors are simultaneously facing managers with performance issues and behavioral problems. Some returning TLE employees are uncommunicative, while others can't stop talking or disturbing others. Some are docile and lack their usual initiative, while others are rebellious and disruptive—even destructive. Some refuse to work, while others work sloppily or make many mistakes. Some are unforgiving, while others are busy punishing themselves.

The third recommendation is the survivor's wish for a "return to normalcy." This is, of course, what everyone wishes for. But the fact is that the workplace situation with a newly returning TLE employee is not normal. And, to most managers, the path to normalcy is unknown. Besides, that path may take different twists and turns for each returning survivor.

A LARGER PERSPECTIVE

The idea of *putting out a welcome mat* for a returning TLE employee reflects a very basic human need. The psychologist Abraham Maslow identified a pyramid of five basic need levels, without which a full human life cannot be lived. At the base of the pyramid, the most fundamental of all needs are the physical and physiological ones, such as air, water, food, clothing, shelter and the touch of another human being. Without all of these, a person would soon get sick and might even die. This first level is essential and a requirement for all the other ones in the pyramid of needs.

The very next level include the needs Maslow described as "safety and security" needs. Unless a person feels safe and secure, no matter how plentifully their physical needs are being met, they remain anxious and fearful for their life, health and well-being. We are a nation preoccupied with safety and security. Not only are our homes locked, bolted and burglar-alarmed, but they and the possessions in them are insured against flood, fire, wind, rain and theft. We take out insurance for liability, disability, health care, hospitalization, retirement, and long term care. We have national programs for Social

Security and Medicare. We also feel the need to be safe and secure wherever we happen to be—in our homes, our cars, shopping malls, elevators, airports and the building where we work.

While physical safety at work is of primary importance so that no harm comes to our bodies, emotional and financial safety is also important to us. One who is unwelcome in a certain place is not likely to feel emotionally safe there. Being greeted with scowls, giggles or, worst of all, indifference does not make one feel safe. Often, Study Circle participants can easily begin the first session by identifying ways they could make a returning TLE employee feel *unsafe*. From these examples, they begin to recognize what *not* to do to help with the recovery process from a traumatic life experience.

You can't expect a returning worker to begin directing his or her efforts for the company in creative, efficient and effective ways until that person feels safe and secure in the workplace. Until then, you can be certain the employee, consciously or unconsciously, will be testing to see whether the office environment is emotionally safe. There is a very simple rule about human energy that says *energy follows attention.* Wherever your attention is focused, there's where your energy will be directed. If you are frightened or feel insecure, your energy will be primarily directed at self-protection and safety and not at the work that needs to get done.

Almost all managers in the Study Circles I have facilitated agreed that there are two essential factors in providing safety—one emotional and one financial—that, if provided, would go far to reduce stress for any returning TLE employee. One was to provide a place where a TLE employee could go and no one would bother him. The other was the assured continuance of their salary or wages.

Notice that this financial "welcome mat" assures the employee that physical needs, the most basic needs of all according to Maslow, will be covered; there will be enough money to pay the bills for food, water, clothing, shelter and medicines. The emotional "welcome mat" begins to cover what Maslow calls the need for safety and security.

But, aside from these two provisions, most managers shake their heads and wonder what other good things they can do for the employees in their charge. That's where the Study Circle proves its value.

CONFLICTING VALUES

Observations from the first session show some managers hesitate to take responsibility for a returning TLE employee. As far as they are concerned, caring for a TLE employee's recovery is someone else's job. Some managers realized they can send the TLE employee to the Employee Assistance Program or to a professional counselor for therapy. Once they have made the professional referral, some managers feel that they have taken care of their responsibility.

In one Study Circle, some participant managers said they hesitated to get involved with TLE employees on an emotional level. They claimed they did not have the professional skills to help, they did not want to interfere with the therapist's work, and they felt that the amount of hands-on time needed to nurture the employee back to normal would jeopardize other work assignments that had to be completed.

However, in the second session of that Study Circle, I presented each one in the group with a photocopied page of "notes from the previous session." After reading the notes about *putting out a welcome mat*, the group quickly clarified a short list of what others in the workplace could do for a returning TLE employee. Most of the items on that list would take very little time to do yet would still be very helpful.

During the first Study Circle session on creating a "welcome mat" for the returning TLE employee, managers typically acknowledge having two colliding values, one that favors compassion, and the other that favors productivity. On the one hand, managers say, "We are responsible for the 'bottom line' and getting the work done. So, even though we feel concern for the traumatized person, we are conflicted about spending precious work time tending to a TLE employee."

After a first session, one employee told me how amazed he was that managers were making such a hard call on performance for a returning TLE employee. He had personally experienced a very uncomfortable transition upon his return to his job. "Because of my trauma it was very difficult to concentrate on my work when I returned, he said. Fortunately, I didn't have the kind of manager who got on my back about work quotas," I encouraged him to share his views with the group during the next session, if and when he felt comfortable.

Usually, all the managers attending a Study Circle agree that, at first, the returning TLE employee should be "acknowledged" when he returns to the workplace. Once, a TLE survivor in the Study Circle group responded to such a remark by saying, "Acknowledgement is good, but we survivors need more than that. Use common sense. Treat us as you would like to be treated if you were in our shoes."

After the first session, two of the male managers and a female employee were demonstrating to each other how they relate to their returning TLE employees. They said that when it's appropriate they liked to give a hug to people when they welcome them back to the workplace. They chose to be demonstrative and touching.

HOW COULD THEY KNOW?

Most managers feel unsure how to approach a returning TLE employee. This is no surprise because no one has ever told them how to do it in a way designed to be helpful to the trauma survivor's emotional recovery. Whatever they did, helpful or unhelpful, they did intuitively.

When I was doing my doctoral research on the topic of traumatized employees and how they fared when returning to their jobs, I found almost nothing in the professional literature, other than how therapists were learning to deal with clients suffering from post-traumatic stress. What could be done in the workplace by managers and co-workers to understand the emotional recovery from the trauma appeared to be an unexplored area. That is why I am writing about what I learned and experimented with. I want to fill in that missing place in the care of traumatized people who find themselves back at work, yet still in the process of healing and adjusting.

During the Study Circle sessions, managers almost universally express a need for guidance on how to tell the co-workers about the returning TLE employee, how they themselves are to negotiate with the TLE employee about work assignments, and how to create a workplace environment that is not threatening for the returning employee.

A few years ago, a civil rights manager in my office told me that he received a phone call from a Director of a government agency that some of his employees were experiencing a variety of traumatic life events and that he, the Director, felt helpless in not having any program available to help his line managers cope with returning TLE employees. The civil rights manager in my department said he shared his Study Circle experiences with the agency Director and was pleased to be able to offer suggestions to him.

Many managers of large corporations or organizations agree that their enterprise probably has many professional resources available to returning TLE employees, e.g., training, counselors, workshops, etc. However, managers are often not aware of the extent of these programs. They will also probably agree that an informational program should be officially provided so that managers know how to ensure that employees get the best available professional assistance when they are dealing with recovery from traumatic incidents.

Here is a sketch of one Study Circle participant named Winston. It is the story of a powerful manager and how he learned about workplace trauma.

WINSTON'S PERSONALITY

Winston volunteered to participate in the Study Circle sessions even though he had never experienced a personal trauma. During my pre-Study Circle interview with him, his only recollection of anything like a traumatic experience was second-hand and it happened with predictable regularity. His wife came from a very close-knit family, and when they returned home from a visit to her family home in South Carolina, it would take her days to readjust to life without them. It was "traumatic," he said, for her to leave them.

Winston is a large man of 45. An African-American with an effervescent personality. He has black wavy hair and his wardrobe is the envy of every other manager in the entire company. He is stylish in every sense of the word and his style matches his extroverted personality. He wears pastel shirts with cuff links and always wears a silver bracelet on his right wrist. This bracelet holds much personal significance for him since he bought it in Mexico and watched as the silversmith created it for him.

Winston was born in 1951 in Alabama in a town about 30 miles south of Mobile. Because his dad was in the army, they moved around a lot and he considered himself an army brat. Winston thrived on the variety, stating, "Every three years I had a new home, new experiences and met new people. It was an adventure." However, he spent the longest time in the Norfolk,Virginia area, where he returned to work as an adult.

His parents have been very influential in his life. He describes his father as very organized and conscientious, his mother as very outgoing, and a person who makes friends easily. His mother's keen sense of style, fashion and skill helped her establish her own business in cosmetology. Although she was not formally trained, she ran her business from their home successfully. Her friendliness always did very well for her. Winston described his mother as a "really classy person." Like his mother, he exudes friendliness and is consequently very well liked in his department. Winston has two sisters and a brother. One sister lives in Baltimore Maryland, the other in California, and his brother lives in Charlotte, North Carolina. He was a middle child.

When you meet Winston, he seems "larger than life." He spends a lot of time on the phone negotiating and talking with colleagues and the general public. His supervisor suggested that I invite Winston to participate in a Study Circle I was facilitating in the Norfolk Virginia area. When I approached Winston, he agreed to come before I could explain what the Study Circle would entail. During the sessions, he was often the first to speak out and get others involved in a dialogue about the topic. He affirmed employees whenever they shared their trauma stories, and took the risk of asking managers very sensitive questions about their own personal traumas. In the Study Circle, he played the role of catalyst and everyone seemed to respond to his disarming manner. He loved to challenge, ask questions and propose taking a different path to a solution. He was the only manager who outwardly disagreed with the group's consensus on topics. Surprisingly, instead of setting people in opposition, this created more energy in the Study Circle, because the group then seemed to participate in a more active manner by asking new questions and probing for more information.

Winston started his career with a large government agency as a Budget Officer then soon moved into a position that spanned several government agencies. He considers himself a policeman for his agency's budget process. He is asked to do things others do not want to do. When his mentor retired, he applied for his job and got it. He has been in his present job since 1998.

Winston has three children—a daughter Penny from his first marriage and two sons from his second marriage, Pelman and Price. His current wife decided to quit her job when she married Winston, to be a traditional mother. When I asked about the divorce from his first marriage, Winston said he did not consider it a trauma. I wondered if there were other traumas in his past.

In 1961 when Winston was a teen, his family moved from Kansas to the Navy base in Norfolk, Virginia. Winston was to be part of the first group to be integrated into the nearby high school. Out of 1,500 students in the school only five were African-American—a natural setting for some traumatic experiences. He was in the 11th grade at this time, he said, and adjusted very well. He joined the basketball and football teams in the 12th grade and became co-captain of both teams. He states that he still goes to reunions with his friends and they talk about how it felt to all of them to handle the issue of integration. Winston says he is not intimidated by racism. "It exists, and we as a people and a society should deal with it."

WINSTON'S EXPERIENCE IN THE STUDY CIRCLE

As the only one who had not experienced personal trauma, Winston said he truly felt blessed compared to people who had no choice in the way some terrible events unfolded in their lives. Winston said he knows of people who just give up, but he proudly announced he did not observe anyone in the Study Circle who had done this. He told participants in the Study Circle they were his heroes, because they had not walked away from their trauma and pain, he said, but had become better people for it.

I watched Winston as other people were telling their trauma stories. He remained quiet and pensive, almost reverent. One employee, Jim, described being part of the Long Island Train disaster of 1993 where a deranged man stood in the aisle of a passenger car and shot bullets in every direction. Telling us the story, Jim said he crawled under the seat and, in complete shock, stayed there until the shooting stopped and police came. Winston was the first person to ask Jim questions as to how he felt when he returned to the workplace as a TLE employee. This question allowed Jim to elaborate his feelings in detail, which stimulated the dialogue among the rest of the participants.

Winston told the group that he had watched the trial of that shooter on television and could, even today, describe the event on that train in very graphic details, but when he realized that he was hearing an eyewitness report in the Study Circle, this overwhelmed him. While watching the trial on television, Winston said he had gotten very angry at the shooter and wished him dead. But now he said he admired Jim retelling his terrifying experience without any malice for the man who almost killed him. Jim's story had a strong impact on Winston. He felt the Study Circle group had allowed him to see beyond his own situation in life. The group gave him "balance" in his thinking, and that was refreshing to him.

WINSTON'S EXPERIENCE WITH TRAUMA
AFTER THE FIRST STUDY CIRCLE SESSION

During the week between the first and second Study Circle sessions, one of Winston's employee's came to him and told him she had cancer. He could tell she had been traumatized by this unexpected announcement from her doctor. The situation was confusing to Winston, because this same person had recently filed an Equal Employment Opportunity complaint against him, and he did not know what to do about it. Winston was faced with an inner conflict that had to be resolved. He approached the situation, as he told us at the next session, in a "clinical manner." He felt that the EEO complaint was going to be resolved by the standard procedures within the system, and he was ready to accept the decision that the system would give him.

However, dealing with the traumatized employee was totally different. It was something new for him. Winston states he remembered the suggestions and ideas he had learned from the Study Circle's first session. He tried to put out a welcome mat for her by allowing her the necessary leave for her treatments. He assured her he was there for her if she wanted to talk and would do all that he could for her in this crisis.

Winston said the discussion in the Study Circle helped him take a caring approach in dealing with his returning TLE employee. He had listened to other participants talking about their supervisors and their often-thoughtless treatment of traumatized employees and, as a result, had become more sensitive to his TLE employee with cancer. Up to this point, he had always been a bottom-line manager concerned with productivity and output, so he seldom allowed people to get extensions on work assignments. Now, with his newly learned attitudes, he was confronted with a totally different situation, one with which he never had dealt, approving sick and annual leave in advance for someone who was really trying to hurt him as a manager. He said the Study Circle put a lot of these issues into perspective for him.

Winston said that the presence of employees in the Study Circle helped him understand what the returning TLE was dealing with internally. Hearing employees share their trauma stories would help him put his workplace requirements in perspective and offer this TLE employee—and future ones—more of a welcome mat than he previously would have done.

Winston is an interesting personality study because he seems to be one of those people who pass through life untouched by traumatic life experiences. For example, while many military "brats" have been traumatized because of continual uprooting of their home life and friendships, Winston found frequent moves an adventure. Again, during the difficult times of racial integration, when many teen African-Americans were traumatized by cruel treatment from whites in these schools, Winston seems to have passed through it all, not merely unscathed but coming out on top as co-captain of two varsity sports teams. And again, when one of his employees filed an EEO complaint against him—his first, by the way—he could have experienced this as a TLE, and many in his position would have, but he did not.

As I mentioned in an earlier chapter, psychologists have noticed that people who have adversely responded to traumatic events early in life are more likely to be traumatized by potentially traumatizing events in adult life than people, like Winston, who had not been traumatized by events in childhood. The point is that when different people are faced with the same potentially traumatizing event, one many be traumatized by it while the other may not. One becomes a returning TLE employee who needs help and support through recovery, the other is simply an employee who has had to face a difficult situation and becomes a better person for it.

Instead of being brought down traumatically by the EEO complaint against him, Winston seemed more concerned with helping the woman readjust to the workplace. He did not brush off the hurt that her complaint brought him. It was simply something difficult for him to deal with. But, it was not a trauma for him. Interestingly, what he found more challenging was discovering ways to understand the emotional recovery process for the woman. Before the Study Circle, Winston would have been concerned about the woman's lack of productivity, but now he became concerned about the three stages of her emotional recovery that were discussed in the Study Circle—not from the cancer itself, which he can do nothing about, but from the trauma of the announcement of it and the changes it has brought about in her sense of self.

Winston says, "It is difficult coping with my TLE employee with cancer. I did okay with the welcome mat thing, but I can't seem to completely reconnect her to the workforce. I don't know what to do. I have tried to talk with her about her trauma, but she refuses to discuss anything with me. I think she has come back to the workplace with a victim mentality. My employee has cancer but also because she has not resolved the issues that made her bring the EEO complaint against me."

Regarding the complaint, which he feels is unfounded, he says, "I've got to put the past behind me and move forward. But, thanks to the Study Circle, I can at least help this woman put her trauma in perspective and become a better person for it."

AN ELEMENT OF POLICY AWARENESS

The Study Circle can serve as a healthy catalyst for a manager's attitude toward a returning TLE employee. The manager is typically the first person to greet the trauma survivor when he or she returns to the workplace, and the manager plays a key role in forming a good relationship with that person upon their re-entry. It is here, on the first day back, when the manager can derail a potential adverse action or grievance. The manager who establishes good communication patterns will eliminate unnecessary performance problems with the re-entry employee. By giving the returning TLE employee a listening ear and acknowledging his return, this type of behavior will create strong credibility with an employee and help the emotional recovery process. Here are a few suggestions that Winston's group offered:

1. Acknowledge the TLE employee's presence when they come back to work. A suggested greeting might be, "I am glad you're back to work. How are things with you? What can I do to help you?"
2. Offer a listening ear. Show the returning TLE employee that you are interested by practicing active listening skills.
3. Body language plays an important part. Watch for behavioral cues from the returning employee, and watch your own behavioral signals. One impatient gesture from you will nullify all your compassionate words.
4. If a TLE employee does not want to talk to you, suggest that they talk to a colleague or someone at work that they trust.

SOME DOS AND DON'TS

After years of conducting Study Circles on understanding the emotional recovery from trauma and from reading many related books, I have developed a list of Dos and Don'ts in dealing with survivors of trauma who return to the workplace to start their work lives over. Some of these suggestions have already been mentioned, but I thought it helpful to put them together in one place. Studies show that traumatized people often benefit most from talking with family and friends. As Sheryle Baker, Director of The Life Center of the Suncoast, Inc., Tampa, Florida, mental health counselor and trauma expert, says about recovery from trauma, "It all begins with a conversation." Here are some of the best ways to reach out to returning TLE employees:

Don'ts

Don't avoid them or leave them feeling abandoned.
Don't be afraid to ask how they are doing.
Don't invalidate their feelings by saying things like "Cheer up" or "Stop crying."
Don't brush off the incident or encourage them to "just forget about it."
Don't tell them to stop complaining and get on with their lives.
Don't tell them they're lucky it wasn't worse.
Don't take their expressions of anger or other strong reactions personally.
Don't try to impose your own opinions about why the trauma happened.

Dos

Reassure them they are good people and that you care about them.
Show them that you care by hugging them or holding their hand.
Sit with them quietly and show empathy—your presence is important.
Share your own feelings (not opinions) about the traumatic experience.
Be prepared to just listen and say nothing.
Allow them to go through their grieving process at their own pace.
Encourage them to take advantage of assistance services.

Chapter Eleven

Lending a Listening Ear: The Second Study Circle

DEVELOPING SENSITIVITY

A Study Circle facilitator can never predict how individual participants will work together in a group setting or react to each other. All you can count on is they will all be interested in the topic of how to deal with employees returning to work after a traumatic life experience.

This second Study Circle session, because of its topic, *lending a listening ear*, creates a bond among participants mainly because most of them, managers and employees alike, have themselves experienced trauma and the difficult return to work. And if they haven't experienced a traumatic life event personally, they have managed or worked beside someone who has. But even when participants, like Winston in the previous chapter, have neither experienced a trauma nor supervised a returning TLE employee, they will admit, like Winston, that the sessions "enhanced my sensitivity towards a traumatized employee."

SECOND SESSION

The theme of the second session in the Study Circle on understanding the emotional recovery of trauma is *lending a listening ear* so that the returning TLE employee feels free to tell the trauma story and experience.

Some of the discussion questions proposed on the participant handout for this session are:

What would it mean to you to "lend a listening ear" to the returning TLE employee to tell his trauma story?

Are there ways, verbally or nonverbally, to "not allow" such employees to tell
their story, even if they wanted to?
Are there ways you could allow the person to tell their trauma story that
would not be helpful in the person's emotional recovery?
Do you know how to use "active listening skills" with the TLE employee?

Sometimes persons who have suffered a trauma have been so shocked
by it that they find it difficult to recall the event at all or they remember
only parts of it. Even when the trauma is vivid in their minds and even
though it would be psychologically helpful for them to talk about it, they
are reluctant to do so and find themselves avoiding people who would
encourage them to talk. After all, if you had been raped and beaten, would
you be eager to talk about it to co-workers? Or if your husband had run
off with another woman because he said he was bored with you, would
you feel comfortable sharing the details of your traumatic experience with
the person who works at the desk next to you? So, allowing and inviting
the traumatized employee to talk about their traumatic experience is not a
simple matter.

Some traumatized people are tempted to drinking, brooding and blaming
themselves for the traumatic incident. Depending on the trauma, survivors
may feel degraded, shamed, humiliated, helpless, isolated, in pain, fearful,
anxious, angry, resentful, or some other unwelcome feeling. It is safe to say
that there is probably much emotional turbulence in a returning TLE employee. They may need to get it out somehow, hopefully in a non-harmful
way. Talking it out with the right kind of person almost always helps.

RESPECTING PERSONALITIES

In the second session, I find most participants are open and spontaneous. I
had one group in which participants during that session recounted 14 different
traumatic stories. They told about their trauma experiences, gave each other
feedback, and shared their philosophy of life. They discussed the importance
of respecting a person's personality and culture during the re-entry process.
They observed that some individuals were introverts and some extroverts,
and that this aspect of a person's personality influenced whether they would
be open to talking about their trauma.

They also observed that some individuals may have been brought up not to
talk about personal matters to anyone outside their family. Such people, they
said, might not feel comfortable sharing an intimate side of their personality
with a co-worker. All participants agreed that, if returning TLE employees

choose not to share their painful experiences, managers and co-workers should honor this wish. So a listening ear is not a demanding ear.

In contrast, I once had a group who found it hard to focus on the telling of their own trauma stories, even though I began the session by telling about a trauma event in my own life. After I finished and no one spoke, I asked an employee participant to tell her trauma story. When she finished, the group complimented her. As part of her story, she said she had been grateful that, when she first returned to work after the event, her boss had encouraged her to talk about her traumatic event. The group affirmed her for risking letting her story be known in the workplace and told her that her boss had excellent listening skills.

One participant, who sat across the table from her with his hands folded in a closed position and complimented her on her courage in telling her story, did not offer to tell his story, which I knew was a powerful one, as he had told it to me during his pre-Study Circle interview. The focus of this group seemed to be not on telling their own trauma stories, but on how they believed managers should act responsibly in dealing with returning TLE employees. They seemed more focused on the political environment of the organization than on the individual's story.

You can never predict the direction a group will take; you can only be sure that it will be interesting and exciting. Their stories certainly are.

TONY—A CASE STUDY IN THE EFFECTS
OF A PERSONAL TRAUMA

Tony's story shows how unaware our organizations are in general in understanding and dealing with individuals who have experienced a personal trauma in their family and are returning to the workplace. I was able to study how this manager tried to function in two worlds—his professional life and his personal family life—over a period of two years. I was able to observe Tony not only during Study Circle sessions but also to listen to him reply to personal questions in an interview. Using this two-level observation process I was able to follow his story from the beginning and gain new perspectives on trauma and some specific needs an individual has when he returns to the workplace.

THE ORGANIZATION AND TONY'S PLACE IN IT

Tony Tonatello works as a senior officer in a government agency in a branch office in Cincinnati. The employees who work at this department represent

America's full ethnic, social, cultural, religious and educational diversity. The mid-west is the hub for all major social programs sponsored, funded and observed by the federal government.

Tony has been employed by the government for 26 years. He is a white Anglo male, 52 years old, medium height with light grayish brown hair. A handsome man, he sports a mustache and wears frameless glasses.

Tony was born and raised in Brooklyn, New York. His ancestry is Italian, and he speaks with a Brooklyn accent that contrasts with his Oxford button-down collar and navy blue blazer look. He was raised Roman Catholic and grew up in a big family with parents who placed a high value on hard work, education and an active church and community commitment.

He came to Washington in the early 60s, obtaining his first job with the Census Bureau. He also worked with a private corporation and then relocated to the central part of the country. Once settled in Washington, he married Celeste, his high school sweetheart, and together they raised five children. At the time I met Tony in Cincinnati, his oldest child was 27, his youngest 16.

TONY'S WORLD TURNED UPSIDE DOWN

Tony's trauma story began in August, 1989, with a telephone call from Dr. Granger of the City Hospital in Cleveland, informing him that his daughter Melody, who was 15 years old at the time, was diagnosed with cancer. Earlier that month, Melody had found some lumps near her collarbone and brought them to her parents' attention. After two weeks, they seemed to get larger. Tony took her for an examination, and a biopsy identified the cancer. The doctors performed an emergency laparotomy and splenectomy. The cancer had not spread, they said, and she then began six months of chemotherapy treatments and ten days of radiation.

Upon hearing the diagnosis of his daughter Melody, Tony told me, his priorities immediately changed. No longer was he concerned about advancing his career and status or earning a lot of money. None of these any longer seemed important to him. His total focus was on his daughter and her well-being, and trying to figure out what to do. Like the good analyst that he was, Tony immediately began to research her illness through the available medical school libraries in his area. He even made trips to the National Institute of Health in Bethesda, Maryland. In a short time, he became an expert on her illness, her drugs and her treatment.

Because Tony's wife was an elementary school teacher and could not take time to escort their daughter to the doctor appointments, Tony took care of everything.

During these months, Tony's days were erratic. He lived a dual life. He had to be there for his daughter, and he had to go to work. He said he did not function very well at the office. He told his superior of his trauma and, compassionately, the superior told him to do whatever he had to do. Although the superior took care of Tony's schedule needs, such as allowing him to use annual leave time whenever he had to care for his daughter, Tony realized his emotional needs were not being met. He had nowhere to go to talk out his feelings. He said he did not even know how to express his feelings. He said, "My heart was ripped in two and my whole body ached." As a father, he wished he could spend all his time supporting his daughter and do nothing else. But even in trying to help her, he felt powerless.

THE MANAGER'S RESPONSIBILITIES

In the second session you can expect to hear differing comments about how managers should interact with TLE employees. Logistically, Tony's superior was good to give him time off without making a fuss and to go easy on his work requirements, but emotionally and in empathy the superior didn't score very highly.

Second session discussions usually affirm the importance of the TLE employee's personality and the need to allow for a variety of performance expectations upon their return. All will agree that managers should give work assignments to returning TLE employees gradually, allowing the employee to familiarize slowly when returning after a trauma. Managers among the participants will also agree that understanding about introverted and extroverted personalities would help them in understanding their employees, but they may point out that managers also have different personalities—"Some of us are outgoing, others are aloof and cool."—and managers need to understand themselves, too. Perhaps Tony's superior was an introvert and had a hard time dealing with heavy emotions in someone else. Tony, himself a manager, acknowledged that, before the Study Circle, he wasn't much good in empathizing with returning TLE employees.

Managers in a Study Circle group who themselves have returned to work after a traumatic experience are usually more sensitive to the needs of a returning TLE employee. But there is no guarantee that this transformation will happen. Some managers may acknowledge how, "My trauma changed me. I have learned to use my wounding experience to help someone else in their pain." And "I feel free to approach a returning TLE employee and let them know I'm available." It didn't happen to Tony as a manager until he experienced the Study Circle. As much as he wanted and needed empathy from his superior, he seemed unable to offer the same to those traumatized people he himself managed.

Most groups recognize that individuals who are returning to the workplace after having experienced a trauma ought to be acknowledged by someone in the organization, preferably their manager. This manager should ask the returning employee what her colleagues can do for her. Groups will also usually advise managers to watch for cues from the employee about how to respond, and not to intrude if the person is unwilling to share their feelings at work at this time.

Knowing how to give a referral for professional care and knowing where to send a TLE person returning to the workplace after the trauma was seen by all groups as an essential skill for any manager. For some reason, Tony's superior seemed to have missed this opportunity completely. He was never referred for counseling. "But, then again," admitted Tony, "neither did I refer my survivors for counseling before I did the Study Circle."

There's more to Tony's story.

TONY'S WORST FEAR REAPPEARS

This trauma with Melody went on for a year and a half. Finally, in the early spring of 1990 Tony and his family were told that treatment had worked and his daughter had become 95% free of the cancer. But they recommended Melody continue going for tests every month. Life in Tony's family slowly began to return to some sort of normalcy.

Unfortunately, in September of 1990, Tony received another phone call from Dr. Granger stating that the doctors and specialists had run two sets of test on Melody, and they confirmed that the cancer had spread to her lymph nodes and areas around her heart.

When Tony got that phone call at his office, he said he froze at his computer. He felt paralyzed. He could not focus. He checked his watch and it was close to noon. He left the office to attend lunch hour mass at a Catholic church nearby and pray for guidance.

After the congregation left the church, he sat there in a daze for two more hours trying to compose himself and think of how he and his family would get through this ordeal. He still had to go home to tell his wife Celeste and daughter the bad news.

As he sat in the church pew, Tony said he was angry at God. He asked God, "Why me? Why us? Why my daughter? Why are we going through this again? Why are we being punished? What did we do to deserve this?" Tony wasn't sure how he would ever collect himself to be able to talk to his family.

When Tony arrived home, he called his wife and daughter together and told them about the phone call he got from Dr. Granger. They all held each other and cried.

The doctors did not want to perform surgery, so they immediately began the treatment again. Tony's nightmare only got worse. He had to go to Melody's school to arrange for her to be tutored and then talk to the cheerleading coach, since Melody had just made the cheerleading squad. As Tony took complete charge of Melody's care, all types of feelings were welling up inside him. He says, "I felt inadequate. I wanted to make it more comfortable for Melody, and I couldn't. I felt her pain and wanted to take her place, and I couldn't."

Tony and Celeste decided to join a support group for parents. This helped them to understand what other parents were going through. Many evenings after leaving the group, they found themselves being thankful they did not have to bear some of the extra complications other parents were experiencing.

Tony said his relationship with his wife at this time was also severely stressed. Being an elementary school teacher, Celeste would come home and would want to talk about her classes. Tony admits that he was not interested in her work; he was totally preoccupied with his daughter's health. Because of this conflict, Celeste sought a counselor to deal with her emotions. The counselor, instead of helping Celeste stay in the marriage, suggested they separate. Celeste returned home and discussed her feelings with Tony, and for the first time they talked about their relationship, their deep love for each other, and their need for mutual support. They ended up staying together and supporting each other.

At this same time, the other children were feeling the stress of Melody's new bout with illness. Tony's two sons away at college said they had lost interest in their schoolwork and wanted to come home to help the family through this crisis. Tony urged them to stay in school. His younger son Robert said, "I wish I had the cancer and not Melody." Melody's answer to her younger brother was, "I can handle this, but I couldn't if it was happening to you."

RE-ENTERING TONY'S WORK WORLD

Tony's supervisors at the office began asking him to assume more responsibility. He told them, "I cannot handle any more work at this time." He felt he could do only routine tasks, those he was familiar with. He did not want to take on any new policy issues. His supervisors reminded Tony that this refusal to deal with new work had been going on for over a year, since Melody had first been diagnosed with cancer.

Tony said he tried to talk to his co-workers, but found it very difficult to express his feelings. Besides, he was not sure that they cared. In our interview, Tony said, "Some people are comfortable asking for help and some people are not." He was one who was not.

When employees are not good at asking for help, a manager's communication skills become very important.

COMMUNICATION SKILLS

One Study Circle group that focused in their first session on the importance of communication skills about putting out a welcome mat for the returning TLE employee, continued with this topic throughout the second and third sessions. In encouraging managers to develop good "listening ear" skills, they suggested the following:

a. *Develop active listening skills.* These are important when dealing with an individual returning to the workplace after a trauma.
b. *Be cautious* in approaching a returning TLE employee and be sincere in your acknowledgment of them.
c. *Show compassion.* Unfortunately, while some people naturally have compassion, others do not. Nevertheless, it is a quality that should be shown towards a returning TLE employee.
d. *Don't offer false compassion.* It's worse than saying nothing at all to an employee.
e. *Don't try to play therapist in the workplace.* As a rule, besides showing compassion, encourage the employee to go to the Employee Assistance Program for counseling or at least to talk out whatever is troubling him.

A traumatized employee who has a strong religious faith may often turn to a spiritual director for guidance, consolation, and courage to deal with the emotional pain he is dealing with. A manager may find it helpful to suggest that such a returning employee seek support from their church community.

After months of chemotherapy and radiation treatments, Tony's daughter Melody was scheduled to go to the hospital for her first check-up. That same day Tony went to the church and prayed. Some weeks before, he had discovered a book on the lives of the saints. He was especially attracted to the story of St. Solanum Cagey that was entitled "Nothing Short of a Miracle." This saint, who had a healing ministry, had died in the early 1960's. Solanum recommended that one should be thankful first and accept the will of God before praying for healing. Tony began to pray by thanking the saint and said, "If my daughter's cancer is worsening and we could lose her, I want the strength to live with her with this disease." From that day on, Tony continued to pray with the attitude recommended by the saint.

A few days after the check-up, Dr. Granger called Tony and told him that the team of doctors had just completed two tests on Melody, and there was no sign of the cancer at all. He said they wanted to do another set of tests the next week. The following week, the oncologist called Tony and said the doctors from the cancer board reviewed the third set of tests, and there were no signs of cancer anywhere in her body. The doctor told Tony Melody would require no additional treatment, since she was now completely free of cancer.

Tony, Celeste and Melody met with the team of doctors, who could not explain what had happened to bring about the young woman's health. Tony said, "A miracle has happened to our family." The doctors acknowledged they would never forget this case and could not offer a medical explanation.

TONY'S WORLD TODAY

Tony decided to become a Deacon in the Catholic Church and now ministers to others like him who have gone through different phases of trauma. With his career back on track, his work world is busy with assignments and travel. Family life is normal again, too. He and his wife just returned from their first trip to Italy.

By the time I met Tony, two of his sons were married, one daughter was in college and Melody had recently become a bio-medical engineer with her first job at a nationally respected clinic operating the sophisticated machinery and administering to patients who are ill and seeking assistance in their traumatic times. Although Tony and Celeste miss her, they wish her well. A part of them still feels the effects of their own trauma but awe at how their life has unfolded.

During my interview with Tony before the Study Circle began, I asked him how this trauma changed him and his life. He admitted that prior to it he could never talk to anyone about a terminal illness. Now, he is very comfortable in talking and ministering to the sick and dying. But not so much as a manager at work.

We then focused on the workplace, and I asked him if he thought supervisors today were better able to deal with returning TLE employees than they were when Melody was first diagnosed with cancer. He said no. He said most supervisors still avoid employees after a trauma, mostly, he thought, because they do not know how to relate to them. He wished also that teams at work could help people support each other more when a trauma occurs in their lives.

From my observations of Tony in the Study Circle and afterwards, he was a pivotal person in the group. He willingly shared his trauma story, which helped others talk about their trauma. In group dialogue he was very forthcoming and articulate. During the second session, Tony reported that he had gone back to the office and was able to talk more openly and freely to an employee who had just experienced a death in her family.

After the Study Circle, he expressed to the group how he had benefited immensely from others in the group and felt he now knew many new ways he could he helpful as a manager to other returning TLE employees. He thanked me especially because he made a new friend in the Study Circle group; a man who had left the priesthood, got married and began working for the department asked him if they could have lunch.

COMMUNICATION AND GROUP CLIMATE

I usually open each session of a Study Circle by reading notes I have taken from the previous session. This creates an opportunity for group members to refresh their memories on what they discussed the last time. It also gives them a chance to improve or refine what they said then.

At the opening, I might also take the time to comment on the discussion process and re-motivate the group, saying something like: "Last session, our group interaction worked quite well. In the beginning, some individuals dominated the exchange of ideas, but as the session progressed all members became active participants. The main reason for the success of this group is that you all came here to address a specific need. You wanted to help managers and co-workers with the re-entry process of a TLE employee. Every one of you felt the need personally. That's why you work so well together."

When a number of people get together to discuss an issue that is important to them, their attitudes and behavior can create either a defensive or supportive climate. When defensive behavior occurs, individuals perceive themselves being threatened or they anticipate a climate of threat in the group. They feel unsafe and insecure. They feel separate and alone, and they usually withdraw from participating. On the other hand, supportive behavior usually has the opposite effect. They feel safe and secure. People feel close, connected. They want to share and they want to learn from others. They find consensus in their decisions.

In his book, *Ethics in Human Communication*, Richard. L. Johannesen (1990) observed that "supportive communication is essential to a dialogical ethic of group communication; only in this positive climate can people maintain their own values, dialogue openly and make ethically acceptable decisions"[1] (p. 207).

Gay and Tonyald Lumsden (1992) in *Communication in Groups and Teams: Shared Leadership* state that a supportive climate "builds openness, trust and empathy."[2] (p.150) These three elements are interdependent, each contributing and reinforcing the others.

First, regarding *openness* in a Study Circle, supportive participants show a definite interest in the perceptions of others and listen to their points of view. They are lending a listening ear. They also tend to be open-minded. They are willing to risk and generously share their trauma stories. This usually creates a very positive climate of trust.

I recall one employee who shared his trauma story and, in talking, gave insight to what he was feeling about his work, his supervisor and the organization. Others probed further by asking him questions. Elaborating on his own trauma—his teenage son had committed suicide—he continued to take the risk in sharing his insights about what went on inside him emotionally after the event, which helped create trust among participants and allowed members to bond with each other. This bond continued outside the Study Circle. After the second session, some of the members attended a retirement party for a colleague in their department. I noticed some of these participants, previously unacquainted, talking with each other and sharing work experiences at this party.

Deeper understandings of the dynamics of trauma occur in a Study Circle, especially during the second session when participants go into their trauma stories in greater detail. During this session they are all developing a "listening ear."

In their openness in telling their trauma story to the group, they give insights to each other. For example, one young woman who had been raped said when she returned to the workplace after her trauma, she "was there, and not there." She told, for example, how she might be sitting in a staff meeting but her mind and all her attention was back at the scene of the trauma. She explained further that returning TLE employees like her were often "not the same person" when they returned to the workplace, and she described how she saw herself differently since the trauma. She acknowledged that she sometimes feels as if she is a dirty and shameful person, even though she knows in her head that these feelings shouldn't be there.

Second, *trust* in a group setting comes gradually, no matter how supportive participants may be. Trust is built in small increments. For example, in the second session when Tony shared the trauma story of his daughter's cancer, it had a rippling effect of trust within the group. Soon, another manager talked about her son's murder. Each story created another layer of "safe trust" in the group. Soon after that, another manager from the Office of Public Policy shared his trauma. This manager told the group that his son has been in a coma three years because of an automobile accident. Even today, the son is unable to recognize anyone and cannot even squeeze his father's hand. This man asked the group how they could help him deal with his on-going trauma, because it is with him every day. He shared with the group how, in the early months of the trauma, everyone was very attentive to him and his needs, but as time went on not very many people asked about his son. Nowadays at work almost no one ever brings up the topic. The group surged in support of this manager who carried such an emotional burden to work with him every day. But such a story comes out only when the group has built up enough mutual trust to sustain powerful feelings.

The third quality a supportive group builds is *empathy*. Empathy is also a quality that just about every Study Circle group says is needed in managers for dealing with a returning TLE employee. Groups discuss this quality at length, with managers usually admitting not knowing how to show it and asking, "What is it?"

Experts suggest that empathy means learning to understand the values, meanings and symbols of another person. Others describe empathy as "walking in another person's moccasins," or feeling what another person feels. In groups I facilitated many managers were not sure how much empathy they should show the returning TLE employee. But they did realize that productivity in a returning TLE employee would be lower if managers did not deal positively with an employee and his trauma.

I recall one employee who shared in the group his frustration and anger about his supervisor. He told the group members that his son had suffered a head injury and he had to be out of work a month to care for his son. When he returned, his boss never asked about his son. "It's been five years," he said, "and to this date, he has never approached me about the matter." By sharing their trauma stories and their treatment at the hands of unfeeling managers, returning TLE employees give managers a "new lens" to see how an employee actually feels when returning to the workplace and how they view a thoughtless manager.

As I observed Tony in the interview and Study Circle, I recognized a man who was eager to share his experiences with someone. As part of the interactive dynamics of the Study Circle, he was the first person to tell his trauma story. He not only set the tone for other people to talk openly during the second session, he took the biggest risk. He talked about men and their feelings, and "how I struggled every day because no one was available in the workplace to comfort me." Individuals in the group were visibly moved by his story and, as a consequence, others were willing to share their own trauma experiences.

A DISRUPTIVE TLE EMPLOYEE

Sometimes, if a Study Circle group focuses on the issue of "problem employees" during their first session, the same theme will naturally arise in the second session. They may talk about the manager's dilemma and what he/she should do when returning employees either refuse to do their assignments or do the opposite of what they are asked to do.

In one group, they brought up a special kind of problem employee: What does a manager do when the employee not only recounts the trauma story but talks incessantly about it?

One female manager who experienced the loss of her son suggested, "Allow the TLE employee space to discuss the trauma. Don't push them to talk, but don't let their retelling their story become disruptive in the office."

After much discussion, the group suggested the following guidelines for dealing with TLE employees who tend to talk incessantly about their traumatic experience:

a. If a TLE employee by talking incessantly is consuming a lot of their co-workers' time, the manager *must* intercede. One suggestion was for the manager to recommend that the TLE employee see someone in the Employee Assistance Program for counseling.

b. Try to re-focus the talking employee's interest on the task that needs to be accomplished, then in a gentle way, with some diplomacy, try to get him/her back on the work track.

c. Give the returning TLE employee alternate work options where there is less temptation to keep talking. Help everyone in the group to understand that there are different types of trauma and the recovery process may be longer for a specific type of trauma or for certain personalities.

d. When the TLE employee first returns to the workplace, it is important how and when the manager approaches him. An early meeting will usually reveal the employee's special needs and perhaps relieve his need to keep re-telling the trauma story and share his experience with the manager.

SUMMARY

As I continue to facilitate Study Circles on trauma and recovery in the workplace, I am continually impressed by the power of this interactive learning model in bringing individuals together to discuss a sensitive topic about which they all have strong feelings. Tony, in particular, said he had learned new concepts and new approaches while listening to some of the others' responses. He also stated that he learned a lot when managers and employees were trying to come to agreement about the conflict between "empathy and productivity." "During those discussions," he said, "I gained a new perspective about the manager's point of view."

Specifically, Tony recognized through the sharing of another participant, who happened to be a manager, the crucial importance of knowing how to deal with a "volatile employee" since such behavior could seriously affect co-workers in the workplace. When other employees and managers began asking questions on how this situation could be handled, they learned the steps that an individual manager took and the way he talked with the employee. Tony took the initiative to ask the group if guidelines could be set up for managers and employees as a kind of reference tool. He felt this would be helpful.

By the end of the Study Circle's second session, participants have become a powerful interactive learning team. During the third session they learn to *offer a helping hand* and realize the importance of making the returning TLE employee feel like an integral part of the workplace team once again.

NOTES

1. Ethics in Human Communication. (Long Grove, Illinois: Waveland Press, 1990), p. 207.
2. Communications in Groups and Teams: Shared Leadership. (New York: Wadsworth Publishing Company, 1992), p. 150.

Chapter Twelve

Offering a Helping Hand: The Third Study Circle

ON THE OUTSIDE, ON THE INSIDE

I like to call the third stage in understanding the emotional recovery process of the returning TLE employee *offering a helping hand*. Its purpose is to invite the manager and co-workers to take the initiative in restoring their personal and professional connections with the survivor.

On their first days back to work, despite how "normal" TLE survivors may appear on the outside, they often feel disorganized, disoriented and disconnected on the inside. Because of the traumatic event, their sense of trust in others may have been severely weakened, their sense of control over things severely shaken, their confidence toward others in the workplace unsure. For some, their life meaning is falling apart and many question their fundamental beliefs.

As a rule, co-workers are puzzled at the unusual behavior and attitude of a returning TLE employee and, as a result, may show very little support toward the survivor. For various reasons, connections have been broken. The traumatic event itself has done this. A woman who has been raped or a father whose teenage son committed suicide, in their shame and embarrassment or feelings of guilt, may imagine themselves as a dirtied person or a failure as a parent, and so may presume that their co-workers see them in the same way. They may think, "My co-workers won't want to relate to me anymore."

On their own part, co-workers as a rule do not know how to treat survivors. Many fellow employees expect them to have gone for counseling and have gotten "straightened out" before returning to the job. Just as returning TLE employees themselves have difficulty reconnecting with the organization, co-workers are not sure what to do, how to relate to them or suggest where they can go for assistance, if they seem to need it. This is where learning to *offer a helping hand* comes in.

Some reconnection-related questions the Study Circle's third session hand-out asks participants to think about are:

Can you describe some of the kinds of "connections" that typically exist between manager and employee and between worker and co-workers?
How do people in the workplace re-establish such connections after they have
   been broken?
What kinds of questions might you ask the returning TLE employee to help
   re-establish connections?

THIRD SESSION

I often ask participants to rank the three Study Circle sessions they attended in their order of importance. Consistently, they say that the third session—of-fering a helping hand to help the returning TLE employee get reconnected to the workplace community—was the most important. They recognize finally that reconnection is perhaps the most crucial stage in the re-entry process.

I found this final session also to be the most challenging and the most prac-tical for participants, since reconnecting necessarily involves all of the return-ing employee's co-workers. The same is true even when the returning person is a manager, like Tony whose story we reviewed in the previous chapter.

In the third session, manager-participants tend to focus on how to discuss the trauma with co-workers and what tone to set in the organization when the TLE employee returns to the workplace. I recall one male manager who said, "Managers must send out the right signals to the staff." Another added, "We should include the returning TLE employee in staff meetings, and reassure the person that his status has not changed because of the trauma."

MASLOW'S LEVELS OF NEEDS

In Maslow' pyramids of human needs, right after the need for safety and security, the *need to belong;* to be part of some human group is essential to being alive. We all meet this essential need of belongingness in many differ-ent ways: by having a last name, being members of a certain family, having a home where we live and using a room in that house that belongs to us. Each of these things gives us a sense of belonging, of being connected. To further develop this sense of belonging, we connect with others in neighborhoods, extended families, ethnic groups and nations. Isn't the need to belong the reason we frame photographs of family members and display them, to remind us of our connections and the different ways we belong to each other?

Frequently, too, we bond with people in our workplace to fulfill this need of belonging. We identify ourselves as working for "this" company. We have our own desk office that tells the world we belong here. We have personal and financial records and other forms of connection to this organization in the manager's personnel files. We have colleagues, who call us friends and whom we look forward to seeing each day. We also like to say that we belong to a team of productive people doing something to serve society. Work does much more than help us take care of physical needs and safety and security needs. For most of us, it is a place where we, to some degree, shape our identity and our values as well as our contacts and our friendships. The workplace is a place where we often feel most ourselves.

For many, the bonds they form at work are among the strongest connections they have. For these, the workplace is, above all, the place where they feel most connected to others. And when these connections are broken, their re-establishment is a strongly felt need. As such, re-establishing connections is an important stage in the process of emotional recovery from trauma. Full emotional recovery from a traumatic event is often impossible without restoring a human and personal connection to the people at work.

I did not bring up Maslow in the previous chapter because telling the trauma story has implications in at least two or three levels of human needs. Feeling ready to tell my trauma story experience to a manager or co-worker means that I feel that the workplace has provided an adequate "welcome mat" for me. Do I find people ready to lend a listening ear, since telling my story to someone in the workplace is my first test of the welcome mat? If I feel free to tell my trauma story to my manager or a co-worker, which tells me that my safety and security needs are in place.

Telling my story is also a test of the need to belong. When I tell my story, will it be listened to with compassion and concern, as I hope it will be? Do my co-workers accept me as a person who has been through a traumatic life experience? Do they accept me as one of them again? Do they make me feel that I belong?

Maslow identified a fourth level of need we all feel, beyond belongingness and acceptance. It is the need to be approved, to be valued, to be esteemed. It is an old saying that a family has to take in even their worst member because he lives there and belongs there, but it is one thing to live in the house where you belong, and another thing to be loved, valued and esteemed there. The same is true in the workplace. The unspoken question in the back of the returning employee's mind is: "They may have to give me my job back, but will they still like me and value me?" Because of this esteem issue, returning TLE employees often at first will talk about only the surface level of their traumatic experience. This is how they test for safety and belongingness. When they begin telling the deeper details—the angry, shameful, anxious emotions and wishes that are roiling around inside them—they are testing for more than a sense of belonging. They are checking for your approval of them. "Do they disapprove of me or think of me as shameful or a failure? Or do they think I'm really a good person or a good parent and that I did the best I could in the circumstances?"

The important point to remember is that the returning TLE employee has many basic needs to test for and, if necessary, re-establish. So, there is much more going on inside such a person than one might think. There are many questions they seek answers to, and those answers can come only from the survivor's manager and co-workers, especially those whose opinions the survivor most values.

DIFFERENT KINDS OF TRAUMA

In the third session, most groups focus on the topic of the different types of trauma that exist in society. In these groups, dialogue usually continues to flow freely. Managers want to make each other aware of how these different types of traumatic life experiences complicate matters, and they ask for feedback on how to define them and deal with them.

For example, they might ask whether the death of a child or spouse would be more traumatic than witnessing an accident or the loss of one's career. Or they might ask what kinds of traumas take longest to heal? Would a person who had been raped take longer to recover than a person who was shot at in a car during a drive-by shooting? Or which traumatic events tend to change the survivor's personality? Would the survivor of a robbery, mugging and a beating be more likely to have a changed personality than someone who had a major heart attack? Questions like these were usually directed at participants who had experienced different types of traumas.

These questions are extremely important, and they tend to rise most often during the third Study Circle session, because the issue of making an emotional reconnection to the returning TLE employee depends on their answers. The story of Dede underlines the importance of this issue.

DEDE'S STORY

Dede Davis walked into my office for her pre-Study Circle interview. She was a petite, pert and pretty thirty-year-old brunette with a sweet smile. By my guess, she was most men's image of the girl next door. Nothing in her appearance hinted at the horrible traumas this woman had experienced. Almost fifteen years ago, she had come to Washington, DC, from a small Midwestern town, like thousands of other young women, eager to start a career in the big city. Within a year after her arrival in the Nation's Capital she had married, but divorced before their first anniversary. The divorce papers stated "incompatibility" as the reason for the divorce, but the real reason was her husband physically and psychologically abused her. That was traumatic experience number one.

Three years later, she had been raped at night outside her apartment. That day, her boss had asked her to work late and it was dark when she got off the bus for the two-block walk to her front door. She never made it home. That was trauma number two.

She was a spunky person and decided that she would never let herself be raped again, so she began working out during lunch hours at a nearby gym. If she was ever attacked again, she had told herself, she would go down fighting. By now, her interest in men had soured, she said, and she decided she would never marry again. I asked her why. She then related the real story.

Two years ago, ten years after her rape, she was in a restaurant with some other women from the office staff having dinner and enjoying girl talk on a winter's evening. She hadn't been feeling too well all week and told her companions she was going home, since it looked like they'd be chatting there for hours.

As she left the restaurant alone for her car, a tall man from the bar followed her out to the parking lot and began to attack her. I'm sure he expected no resistance from the petite Dede, but she fought back with all the strength she had built up working out in the gym. Nevertheless, her attacker beat and bruised her pretty badly. He hit her ankle somehow in a way that fractured it. At this point, another woman happened to be driving by and, seeing what was going on, began beeping her car horn. However, she did not stop her car or get out. But the man was enough distracted by the honking and headlights for Dede to get into her car and lock the door. She drove out of the parking lot as quickly as she could.

For half an hour she drove randomly through the streets, suspecting that her attacker may have gotten into his car and was following her. In case he was tracking her, she did not want him to know where she lived, so she parked about three blocks from her apartment and ran most of the way home. "My foot felt as though it had fallen off," she said. "I don't know how I managed to run on my fractured ankle. I was screaming with the pain of it. My body must have been pumping adrenaline like crazy for me not to have collapsed in pain on the sidewalk."

"The next morning," she explained, "I awoke all bruised and my ankle was swollen and throbbing. Unfortunately, I decided to telephone the police and tell them what had happened in the restaurant parking lot the night before, and ask for a ride to the hospital to take care of my ankle. Instead of compassion, I got abuse. Their interrogation of me was one more traumatic experience. They asked me questions like "Were you provocatively dressed in the restaurant? Were you giving the man come-on signals? Did he follow you to your car because you asked him to? 'Besides,' they said, 'if this guy was as big as you claimed he was, there is no way you could have fended him off. And, according to the doctors who took x-rays of your ankle, they said there is no way in the world you could have walked, let alone run, three blocks to your apartment.'"

"They didn't believe a word I said," she told me. "They were convinced I was lying. To make matters worse, the police called in a psychiatrist who examined me and decided, like the police, that I was lying and needed to be committed to the psychiatric ward of the hospital. I was in the hospital anyway with my fractured ankle, which was now broken, probably because I ran for three blocks on it. But I was humiliated to be treated as an insane person."

"I telephoned my family in Ohio," she went on, "and two of my brothers came to visit me. I expected that they at least would express some sympathy for me, but in questioning me about the incident, they were as bad as the police. They wanted to know if I had been the instigator of the attempted rape. They asked how I had dressed, how I had behaved in the restaurant, and was I in the habit of getting guys to come on to me. These were my own brothers! They were accusing me a being a seductress and implying I had gotten the beating that I deserved."

When I suggested that her brothers' visit was itself another traumatic experience for her, about her fourth or fifth in a few days, she agreed.

"But that wasn't all," she continued. "I had been working in an office for over a year and had been very well liked for my work and productivity. When Sid, my manager, came to see me in the hospital, he started off by saying he was sorry I was not well. I expected at least he would offer some sympathy for what I had been through. He knew me well enough to know that I wasn't crazy or used to making up stories. But a moment later he told me that I was fired. When I began to object, he held up his hand, as if to tell me there was nothing to say. 'Look, Dede,' he said going out the door, 'it's so much easier to replace you than to wait for you to get better. Don't bother to come back to the shop; I'll have your check mailed to your apartment.'"

Dede is no longer working with that firm. When she finally recovered from her broken ankle and the police had stopped harassing her, she started her life over in a new with the federal government, where she has been working for almost two years.

I asked her if anyone in her new job knew about her traumatic experiences. She said no. I asked if she would be willing to talk about any of them in the Study Circle.

She wasn't sure. She would "test the waters. Maybe in the second or third session, if I get up enough courage to create a dialogue with the participants, I will tell my story."

I assured her she was free to share her story in any way she wanted, completely or partially. "Any one of your traumatic life experiences would be enough to challenge the group," I told her. "Your whole story might even overwhelm them, as it has me."

DEDE TELLS HER STORY

Dede did decide to tell most of her story in the third session. After she finished, the group was quiet for a few moments. During the past two sessions, they had developed strong feelings of compassion for one another. Hearing that she had been dismissed from her job without a thought infuriated them. They expressed anger at the callousness of the police officers who had questioned her, at the psychiatrist who had her committed, at her brothers for blaming her for the mugging. It took a few moments for the group to cool down.

To bring the group back to the third session's theme of reconnecting, I posed a hypothetical question to the group.

"We know that in fact Dede's boss Sid was a scoundrel and couldn't be bothered with keeping her job waiting for her," I began. "But let's imagine he was a good guy. Let's imagine on that first visit to the hospital to see her he created a basic welcome mat, assuring Dede that her job was secure and that the rest of the staff were asking for her and wanted to come visit her. Let's further suppose that when he visited her in the hospital a second time he let Dede tell her story and he listened empathetically. But now, six weeks have gone by and it is time for Dede, the TLE employee, to return to the workplace. What kinds of issues would it have posed for Sid and her co-workers to reconnect with Dede? Let's start by listing the different issues that will affect reconnecting with Dede."

Within a few moments we had identified a number of factors that would influence the reconnecting task facing Sid and Dede's co-workers.

Prior relationships
Returning too soon
The gender issue
Personality changes in the survivor

We discussed each of these issues in turn in general and, specifically, for Dede's situation.

PRIOR RELATIONSHIPS

People in the office reconnecting with a returning TLE employee depends on the relationship the TLE had with his co-workers prior to the trauma. Most participants agreed that the ease of reconnection would depend on these prior relationships. If relationships had been good before the trauma, then the returning TLE employee's transition might be easier. And if prior relationships had been poor, strained or nonexistent, the transition might be uphill all the way.

When we considered Dede's manager Sid as he really felt toward her, we decided it was most likely a nonexistent relationship. Sid saw her as an object, as a replaceable part of his office machinery. To him, she wasn't even a human being who deserved respect, care and protection in her situation. They did not see much hope for a reconnection, since there had been no connection in the first place. Dede concurred in their analysis. She felt as her fellow participants did.

When we considered an imaginary Sid as I had described him—compassionate, caring, thoughtful—it was a completely different story. The group agreed that the reconnection in the workplace would be much easier. In fact, they pointed out that by his coming to the hospital and listening to her trauma story, he had created a *welcome mat* provided a *listening ear* and offered a *helping hand*. In this powerful gesture, he had kept the connection with her. It had never broken.

Dede kept silent through this, but wore a wry smile. It was easier for the rest of the group to re-imagine the story in a positive way than for Dede, since the image of the real Sid was inerasably in her mind.

Dede's co-workers, we decided, with Dede's agreement, would have an easier time reconnecting to her than Sid. But, when someone in the group asked Dede whether any of her friends who were at the restaurant with her had phoned or visited, she replied, "Very few, and never more than once."

Participants wondered why this was so. "Were your co-workers embarrassed?" they asked. "Were they frightened? Did Sid tell them to avoid you? Did Sid make up some story to keep them away? Were they afraid that if they befriended you or talked positively about you at work, Sid would fire them too?"

Dede, of course, did not know the answers to their questions.

Then the group began asking themselves, if they were Dede's co-workers, would they have the courage to remain her friend and confront Sid about his cold indifference in firing her. This was followed by some soul searching.

When I asked the group to explore more broadly the prior relationship theme, one person brought up the flip side of the issue. "It takes two to make a relationship," he said. "What if the manager is a nice guy and the employee surviving the trauma has been a perennial pest? How do managers and co-workers honestly reconnect to someone they'd rather not be connected to?"

One manager added that such co-workers can get stressed out by returning TLE employees, especially if the survivor previously exhibited violent behavior in the workplace or had verbally threatened individuals. He stressed that this was a serious problem that he personally had to deal with. "When complaints come to me from this guy's co-workers," he explained, "I have to deal with the problem. I can't shirk these responsibilities."

As a facilitator, I put his question to the group. I said, "Suppose the returning TLE employee had been a problem employee, a borderline performer, or did not always do his/her work?"

"This could create special reconnection challenges for the manager and co-workers." "But it may also be a wonderful opportunity to establish new and more productive relationships with the problem person."

I encouraged the respondent to develop her thought.

Perhaps, she said, before the traumatic event it was common for managers and co-workers alike to treat this problem person with coldness, annoyance or even outright exclusion from the rest of the staff. Providing a welcome mat in the workplace for such a person and lending a listening ear to listen to them tell their trauma story creates a very different atmosphere from what the returning employee might expect. And in this caring atmosphere the person might be ready and willing to change his behavior.

Someone else agreed with her point. "With returning problem workers, people in the office do not want to reestablish the prior strained relationships," he said, "We'd rather initiate a new kind of relationship."

"But," interrupted a participant who had usually been quiet, "for many of us who have been treated badly by such a person—and I have!—it may be quite difficult to let bygones be bygones."

"But if we don't do it," came the reply, "we can only expect to have problems with this returning TLE employee worse than they were before."

Most groups recognize that, no matter what problems a person may have had as a worker prior to their traumatic life experience, when that person returns after a trauma, that person is different because of his experience in the emotional recovery process. That person is in need of special efforts and understanding from managers and co-workers. Managers must realize that a traumatized employee is a changed person. Even though the TLE person may look the same, talk the same and even dress the same, an inner transformation has happened. And it needs to be recognized and acknowledged by everyone in the office.

One manager, speaking from personal experience, said that the returning employee should be greeted and his absence should be acknowledged. Another manager suggested, "The day a TLE employee returns to the workplace would be an excellent time for a dialogue, in essence, as part of welcoming the employee back to the work environment and helping them feel once again part of a team."

Another manager said she found it very helpful to send emails periodically to TLE employees who were still at home, before they returned to work. She stated that human contact was a priority in cases like these and managers need to know and understand that priority, and to take time to do their part.

RETURNING TOO SOON

The next issue we discussed about the reconnection theme was returning to the workplace too soon after a traumatic life experience. Time is an important factor in the emotional recovery from trauma. Although groups usually ask how long it takes for the returning TLE employee to heal from his trauma, they quickly acknowledge from experience that no one can give an exact estimate of the weeks or months it will take to get over a traumatic life experience—if ever. We all have hopes and expectations in this regard, but usually they are way off the mark.

Dede said it was two years since her traumatic episodes with the mugger, the police, the psychiatrist, her brothers and Sid. "I would like to think that I have recovered from it. I've been seeing a psychologist every week for well over a year, trying to work through the bitterness toward it all. I probably wouldn't have started looking for a job as early as I did, but I was running out of money. Nobody stopped sending me bills just because I'd had a trauma."

"Is that when you started working for the new agency?" I asked.

"Yes," she replied. "And my bosses here have been great. So are my friends in the office. My manager here is everything Sid wasn't."

It would be an ideal world if all managers were compassionate, closely monitored the traumatized employee's treatment and the emotional recovery process and had the power to play a key role in deciding when an employee returns to the workplace after their trauma. But organizational policies and health insurance companies usually have a much stronger voice in this matter.

One manager in the group felt traumatized employees are encouraged to return to the workplace far too soon, well before they are ready to work. "As managers," he said to the group, "we must be sensitive to this too-early-return policy in receiving the employee back to the organization. We're the ones who have to deal with it because we're the ones responsible for the returning person's work assignments."

A female manager who herself had been a traumatized person returning to the workplace—her mother had died suddenly—stated that when she returned after her trauma her supervisor did not hurry her reconnection, and gave her a choice of assignments. "He handed me a paper with a list of activities and meeting schedules," she said, "and told me that when I was ready I could choose to be involved in any or all of these activities. I did go to some of those meetings and though I was present physically I was not there mentally." She said this freedom given by her manager helped her tremendously because she did not feel pressured to perform. "He let me monitor my own emotional state and create my own time frame for getting re-involved in the organization."

Managers especially emphasize that the reconnection process is a lot more difficult than it seems. "The office may be going at a frantic pace, but when an employee is returning after a trauma," explained one manager, "you need to shut out all that is going on in the office, stop completely at least for a few minutes, and be totally focused on the returning employee. And in these first moments of reconnection, you need to be sensitive and creative because every returning employee is different and has different needs. There is no formula that I know of that will work for every returning traumatized employee."

In that same group, another manager added a caveat. "I don't disagree with you," he said, "but I find that a lot of managers tend to over-protect the returning TLE employee, rather than create opportunities for more open dialogue between the survivor and their co-workers. I'm for alerting other staff members in the group when a traumatized person is returning to the workplace and encouraging them to help put out a welcome mat and lend an ear to listen to their stories as well as me. Yes, reconnecting with me, the manager, may be important to the returning employee, but re-establishing connection to each member of the staff is at least as important because the returning person will be spending a lot more time with them than with me."

Near the end of a third session, a manager in a different group said he had a personal situation that was rather unique and asked the group's help. His trauma was ongoing, he explained. His son had been in a car accident and was presently in a semi-comatose state. He visits his son daily and his condition has not changed. This situation has gone on for three years. His supervisors were very helpful in the beginning, but now they do not ask any questions or show any concern for his situation, and its business as usual. He said he would welcome some concerned inquiry from his colleagues. He asked me and the group to consider his situation and think about what he could do. As it was the end of the session, the most the group could offer was its sympathy and compassion. But this manager's problem points to another area of trauma research beyond the scope of my work, the chronic trauma, in contrast to the single traumatic life experience that has been the focus of this book.

THE GENDER ISSUE

One important issue that is often discussed during the third session is the different ways gender might affect coping with trauma. In Dede's group discussing this issue, I asked whether, in their experience, women or men cope better after a trauma when coming back to the workplace.

One employee felt that men did not like to talk about very personal matters in the office, and that they might be more open outside the workplace. She said that after her trauma, a sudden divorce, the men in her car pool showed empathy toward her and talked about some of their own emotional struggles, but *only* in the car. "Once they stepped into the office," she said, "it was all business and they never brought up their personal matters. As soon as we stepped into the office, it was as though they had shifted personalities. At least it was true of the three men in our car pool."

A female manager whose son was killed concurred with her, "My husband keeps his feelings inside. I went to a therapist, who helped me," she said. "But my husband still has not dealt with the death of our son. He's still holding it all inside, and I'm waiting for it to blow." Some men in the group suggested that men tend to internalize their feelings and find other ways to work them out, even though they do not want to talk about their traumas.

Another employee whose daughter had been diagnosed with cancer said his wife went into group therapy but he wouldn't go. However, he agreed to attend with her a Cancer Group for parents. When someone in the group asked why he went to one but not the other, he made a distinction between the purpose of the two groups. He saw the Cancer Group offering guidance, and the therapy group offering support. He said, "Men want guidance, not support. I guess women want both."

PERSONALITY CHANGES IN THE SURVIVOR

During the second session, the issue of personality types is discussed because it affects how willing a returning TLE employee may want to tell their trauma story or experience to a manager or co-workers. Extraverted types often like to process their feelings aloud, so it is more likely that an outgoing person may feel more like talking about a traumatic incident than an introverted one, who prefers usually to process feelings internally. The same emphasis might hold true for a survivor in making reconnections with others in the office.

But the issue that arises in the third session is about internal changes that have happened in the survivor as a result of the traumatic experience. When we asked Dede about this, she said she could only speak for herself, but she certainly had changed. "Actually," she said, "I've changed at least twice during the two years since I was attacked. After the mugging and all the rest that followed, I began doubting myself. Can all of these people really be wrong, I wondered? Is it possible that I am really a lewd person? Do I unconsciously send sexual messages to men? Should I share the guilt in this mugging? Was I somehow asking for it? So, at first I really lost faith in myself and my judgment. I wondered if I should feel shamed and guilty. That was my first personality change. I went from a lot of self-confidence and pride in my accomplishments to being full of doubts. It would have been terrible if I tried to come back to work at the old place then. Fortunately, I began seeing a great therapist who helped me to put things in perspective. I was able to relive the mugging and the days that followed and see that I had acted through those events with a healthy perspective. I had done as well as I could in my own self-defense and self-care. In fact, I was courageous and brave through it all. With this perspective, I was able to slowly re-build a strong self-image. Only then was I truly ready to come back to work—even though I had already worked in the new office for a number of months. Luckily, I was not expected to tell my trauma story at the new place, because nobody there knew anything about it—or me."

SUMMARY

After facilitating a number of Study Circles on trauma and emotional recovery, I am more convinced than ever of the power of this interactive learning format in educating people in the workplace. Managers and co-workers do not have to become psychologists or counselors to be able to aid a returning TLE employee in the emotional recovery process. They can be tremendously helpful with just a little bit of education.

The transformative results of the Study Circle are evident in participants on three levels. They are changed cognitively, attitudinally and behaviorally. In other words, after the Study Circle, they think differently about and how long it takes to recover emotionally from a traumatic event. They have developed different attitudes toward returning TLE employees, and they behave differently toward them.

Cognitively, when participants have finished the three sessions of the Study Circle, they are able, among other things, to identify traumatic life experiences (TLEs) and distinguish a single-event trauma from a chronic traumatic situation. They can describe the three stages relative to understanding the emotional recovery of a trauma that a person goes through. They can identify different levels of basic human needs related to trauma. They can define terms like empathy, emotional welcome mat, active listening, and reconnection. They recognize the influence of trauma on different personality types.

Attitudinally, they are cognizant of the need for patience and timing in dealing with traumatized people. They acknowledge the importance of compassion and empathy, of developing listening skills, and of letting the survivor take the lead. Employees learn about the manager's perspective in relating to returning TLE employees, while managers learn about the co-workers' perspective. Managers hear what other managers have done or not done. Employees who have gone through the returning process tell what they wish their managers had done. An important issue that one participant may forget, another remembers. Together they sift out what approaches they think are helpful and which are not. All this happens in stimulating dialogue in a spirit of openness to learning.

Behaviorally, from each other's experiences they learn easy, simple and direct ways to treat the returning TLE employee. In helping support the person's emotional recovery from trauma, they learn what it takes to *put out a welcome mat* in the workplace, skills for *lending a listening ear* to evoke the trauma story, and practical hints for *offering a helping hand* to re-establish connections with the returning employee. Everyone feels the wonderful energy in the group for wanting to be helpful, for wanting the process to work.

I feel more convinced than ever that the Study Circle can effectively fill an important missing step in the organization's treatment of the returning TLE employee.

Part III

SOME SPECIAL CIRCUMSTANCES

—

Chapter Thirteen

When an Entire Group Is Traumatized, How Do Managers and Employees Cope?

WHEN A GROUP IS TRAUMATIZED

Throughout this book, I have focused on the individual worker returning to work after a personal traumatic life experience. But, what if an entire office staff is traumatized by the same experience? Such a precipitating event might be an office break-in, a deranged and disgruntled former employee on a shooting spree in the office, a secret terrorist incident with biological agents that has produced sickness and death among the staff, a fire or explosion in the building, threatening letters sent to the office, and so on.

If everyone in the office is traumatized by an event, who is there to provide a welcome mat for everyone, to listen to their stories, to reconnect them to each other and to the workplace? This is a very different situation from the case of an individual TLE employee returning to the workplace. But such situations happen. They can happen in a business office, a government building, a post office, a school, a church or a synagogue.

A GROUP TRAUMATIC EXPERIENCE

Charlie was the type of a worker who joked with everyone and made the office a fun place to work. He cut out cartoons and left them on his colleagues' chairs and gave them funny surprise gifts. It was only natural for him, as he did one afternoon, to volunteer to work late to finish a budget project that was due the following morning. Joanne, his co-worker who had edited the draft report, agreed to stay with him to finish the final copy.

As everyone was leaving for the day, both Charlie and Joanne decided to take a break and go for a bite to eat before doing the final copy. The

Grub'n'Pub was just down the street, where office staff often met for happy hour, going-away parties, and holiday toasts. This particular evening, Charlie was feeling pretty good. When he and Joanne walked in, Benny the owner of the Grub'n'Pub led them to a special table. As the piano was playing, Joanne started to sing and turned to Charlie to get his reaction. The first time she turned, he was busy talking to some other people. A few minutes passed and she turned toward him again, still singing. This time Charlie's face was resting on the table. Joanne thought nothing of it, since Charlie always liked playing jokes. She called his name but he did not respond. When Joanne looked more closely, he still was slumped over. When she touched him, he fell to the floor. She screamed! Luckily, a doctor was in the pub at the time. They called an ambulance and rushed Charlie to the hospital. When the ambulance arrived at the hospital, Charlie was pronounced dead.

In the office the following morning, unaware of Charlie's death, everyone was preparing for a staff meeting. It was business as usual. Everyone was ready to hear the budget briefing that Charlie and Joanne had prepared. But neither Charlie nor Joanne was present. Suddenly, the secretary screamed and the Director, Ron Carter came running over to her. He took the phone from her, and it was Charlie's wife on the other end. She told him that Charlie died of a heart attack the previous evening. Joanne had left a message on Mr. Carter's phone mail about Charlie's death, but he had not picked it up.

UNPREPARED STAFF

The sudden death of a co-worker in an office is a traumatic event for all of the employees. Shock is what the employees in Charlie's group had experienced upon hearing the news. Shock is a physical and psychological trauma that lasts much longer than most people realize. It affects a person's normal mental functioning. People in shock see and hear things, but the words and images often do not register. It is during this phase that people need the greatest support. Trying to understand the sheer belief that such an event happened, says psychologist Catherine. M. Sanders (1999) in her book *Grief: The Mourning After: Dealing with Adult Bereavement*, leaves people unable to process the normal sequence of thoughts.

No workplace is truly prepared to deal with the sudden death of a co-worker. A friend has died. Someone with whom you have been accustomed to sit near and share thoughts with day after day has suddenly disappeared. You used to spend eight hours a day chatting, joking, planning, negotiating with him, and this intimate communication is stopped in its tracks. In many ways, a closely-knit work environment is like a family—they have feelings for each other. They bond with each other just as siblings do. They, too, share a closeness that is sometimes hard to define. The employees that worked with Charlie were grief-stricken, immobilized and numb. They tried to seek consolation from each other but a vacuum had been created in the office. Charlie was no longer around to joke with his colleagues.

In their book, *The Art of Condolence: What to Write, What to Say, What to Do at a Time of Loss*, Leonard and Hilary Zunin (1991), say these reactions are normal waves of feelings surfacing, and numbness is replaced by a roller coaster of emotion. Time, talk, tears are the best allies of the bereaved.

First came preparing for the funeral. Mr. Carter, the staff director, called Charlie's wife and, when asked, said he would be honored to give the eulogy. Later that day, he visited with each employee to talk about Charlie and learn how he had interacted with them. At the funeral, the tribute to Charlie was not only moving but also revelatory. Charlie's congregation and family learned things about him and his work relationships that they had never known. Mr. Carter said, "Charlie was more than part of the social fabric of the office, he also was an excellent employee who cared about people." The eulogy emphasized how Charlie's co-workers grew to love and see him as part of their work-family and how they would miss him as people miss close friends. Charlie's wife, very appreciative of their sensitivity, asked Mr. Carter for a copy of his prepared words.

Coming back to work, the staff faced an uncertain terrain no one knew how to navigate. Although the traumatic event had ended, the staff's reaction did not. According to Jon G. Allen (1999) in his book *Coping With Trauma: A Guide to Self Understanding*, "The intrusion of the past into the present is one of the main issues people struggle with as a consequence of a trauma. Memories, flashbacks, powerful emotions all play a part in this process."[1] When the staff got back to the office, for example, Joanne was unable to work. Her imagination refused to stop reliving Charlie's last few minutes at the pub. The secretary began crying as she disconnected Charlie's phone. Mr. Carter gave them both the remainder of the day off.

The rest of the staff had little energy and were unable to work. Charlie's colleagues felt apathy and indifference, as if they couldn't care what happened next. According to psychologist James W. Worden (1991) in *Grief Counseling and Grief Therapy*, such lethargy is not uncommon after a loss. Charlie's co-workers, who usually enjoyed high energy levels, now sat with blank faces trying to decide who was going to inherit Charlie's responsibilities and work assignments. One employee had difficulty coping because on all Charlie's folders he received as his share of office work he found penciled notes as well as doodles of smiling faces. He recognized Charlie's handwriting and it brought back memories. The employees merely coasted the first two weeks after the funeral. Frequently, they would gather in small groups around someone's desk to tell Charlie-stories. Very little work was done.

A few days after the funeral, I had a chance to speak with four of these staff members. Two women shed tears with the mention of Charlie's name and the men wanted me to know what a sensitive and true friend he was to his colleagues.

BEING SENSITIVE TO EMPLOYEE NEEDS

Usually, when a traumatic experience happens to an individual such as a death in the family, the workplace offers the person the opportunity to take bereavement leave and go to the Employee Assistance Program (EAP) Office to get one-on-one counseling. Some organizations even provide debriefing experts to talk with the individuals who have been affected by the trauma. We now understand how, when that person returns to the workplace, managers and co-workers can support and promote the emotional recovery process.

The trauma of Charlie's death provided a similar, but quite different, situation. This was not a case of one survivor returning to the workplace after a trauma, but an entire close-knit team, including manager and co-workers, all of whom considered Charlie a close friend. Who would welcome *them* back to the office, prepare a welcome mat for them and help them readjust?

Mr. Carter, the director, knew of my research, and called to talk about what had occurred in his office. The work he had done with his staff was effective and important, such as participating in the funeral, talking to his employees, being sensitive to their regular workloads and special assignments, and getting extensions on due dates from his own supervisor. He also sent a card signed by each of the office members to Charlie's family along with a book about loss and grief.

I pointed out that each person on his staff, including him, would be called a TLE (traumatic life experienced) employee. Together he and I reviewed the psychological stages of emotional recovery for people who have experienced a trauma and how he and the others there could help each other during their recovery by (1) putting out a welcome mat, (2) lending a listening ear to each other for retelling the trauma story, and (3) offering a helping hand to each other to help everyone get reconnected in their relationships at the workplace. Together, we discussed ways each of these stages could be of help to the staff—at least what he could do.

First, in *putting out a welcome mat*, he declared the office a safe haven for all his employees. He gave time off to those who needed it and did not force people to complete their work. He realized this was no time to be a taskmaster. He allowed them the freedom to choose to go for a walk or take frequent breaks from their normal activities. He met with each staff member to assure them that their work assignment deadlines would be extended.

Second, Mr. Carter encouraged those employees who wanted to tell the trauma story to *lend a listening ear* to each other—or to him. Many of the employees took him up on his offer and stopped in to talk with him about Charlie. At the water cooler, colleagues reminisced and told stories about Charlie and said how much they missed him. Joanne, however, could not seem to talk about Charlie. Because she had witnessed the death of her dear friend and was still in shock, she was unable to share her feelings with her colleagues. One member of the budget team asked her to go for a walk. She purposely didn't ask Joanne about Charlie. Joanne found that to be very helpful.

Mr. Carter felt that he could *offer a helping hand* in getting everyone reconnected, but it would take time. He delayed assignments and decided to honor Charlie's memory by dedicating the staff meeting room to him and naming it in his honor. He decided to have a special ceremony later in the year and invite Charlie's family to join his staff in honoring his memory. He let resuming normal workplace speed up to each staff person. "When you have the energy," was what he said to them. He knew that each person would react differently, and patience was needed to heal this wound. A major difficulty was passing out Charlie's assignments and clearing his office space.

RECOMMENDATION TO ORGANIZATIONS

There are some important thoughts that should be conveyed to managers and organizations when reacting to the death of a coworker when the entire staff is traumatized by the event.

First, it is *not* recommended to have a Study Circle *after* the death of a coworker or manager, certainly not very soon after. Charlie's case is a clear indication of this. The staff's grief is too tangibly present, and because of their state of shock individuals will be unable to participate in and benefit from the group discussions. Returning TLE employees will most likely not yet have processed their grief feelings and will feel invaded if asked in a formal Study Circle session to share any feelings about the loss of the coworker.

In some cases, a professional therapist or social worker may conduct a debriefing session with such a group of colleagues, but a debriefing session with its formal structure is very different from a Study Circle. Also, in observing the traumatized co-workers, if the manager feels the need to suggest one-on-one counseling, they may be sent to the EAP of the organization, or a member of the human resource staff can assist.

Second, I suggest following Mr. Carter, Charlie's managers, example. He talked with all Charlie's coworkers individually. After a few months, workers may be ready to talk about Charlie's death in a Study Circle setting. It is important to allow the office to reintegrate itself emotionally before assembling in a structured educational setting to talk about the loss of their coworker.

Third, a much better idea is for organizations to take a pro-active approach by having a Study Circle on the returning TLE employee *prior* to any traumatic events. In this less emotionally charged context, the managers and coworkers will share past experiences and learn skills from each other on how to respond when and if a traumatized employee returns to the workplace. They would also be better prepared to cope if a traumatic event happened to the whole group.

NOTE

1. *Coping with Trauma: A guide to self-understanding.*   (Washington, D.C.: American Psychiatric Press, Inc., 1995), p. 4.

Chapter Fourteen

How Does an Employee's Trauma Affect His Children?

CHILDREN OF A TRAUMATIZED EMPLOYEE

We usually hear of a traumatic life experience (TLE) happening directly to an individual, but its powerful effects may radiate to others. These others may be colleagues or co-workers as when someone is attacked in the office building where they work, or someone is unexpectedly dismissed from a job. More often, however, a personal trauma, whether it happens at work or elsewhere, is likely to have a strong effect in the home, touching all members of a family, especially the younger children. Psychologists are discovering that children are easily upset emotionally by a traumatic event experienced by a parent or sibling, yet may not show it directly or overtly. This appendix offers some perspectives on this issue.

Although what happens to children after a parent is traumatized is not explicitly the responsibility of people in the workplace, it may be helpful for managers and other employees to know the kinds of things that may be going on in the children of a TLE employee returning to work. Because a traumatic life experience puts unusual stress on the person's entire family, this knowledge may be helpful in giving support, in knowing what to expect or watch for in a child's thoughts and behavior, and in knowing what to say and what not to say to the parent. It's also important since the returning TLE employee may need extra time off and support in helping their children process the traumatic events and deal with their own feelings or reactions. For example, the parent may need to personally take the child to school for a time and pick the child up after school.

Psychologists tell us that when a child's parent or sibling dies, either naturally or accidentally, a number of thoughts are likely to occupy the child's mind.

First, *the child may somehow feel responsible for the death of the family member.* This may seem strange, but psychologists remind us that the child's mind is not logical. Some children believe that wishing for something makes that thing happen. So, children may think that the death happened because they had angry feelings toward the person who died, or that the death was punishment for certain bad behaviors they did, or that there was something they could have done to prevent the death, especially if the death was accidental.

Freddie's mother was killed in an auto accident driving him to school. So, not only was eight-year-old Freddie a witness to her death, he also blamed himself for her death because he was late getting dressed that morning and his mother had to hurry to get him to school. If he had been on time, he told himself over and over, his mother would still be alive, and therefore her death was his fault and he is to blame. Children like Freddie need to be reassured that they were not responsible for the trauma and, in his case, that he was not driving the car or in charge of how his mother drove. He needs to hear that her death was not his fault.

Jennifer's grandfather lived with her family and was dying of cancer. Frequently, she would get angry at him because he complained a lot and snored loudly at night keeping her awake. He died during a night when, earlier that evening, 10 year-old Jennifer had angry and hateful feelings toward him, wishing he were no longer in their house. She felt sure her anger was really a wish for his death, and she concluded that somehow she had caused his death and was responsible for it. Jennifer needs to know that her feelings and wishes did not cause her grandfather's death, which nothing she did or didn't do could have made things come out differently.

When children have guilty thoughts like these after a traumatic life experience has happened to someone close to them, children need to be reminded, perhaps again and again, that:

a. They were not at fault.
b. There was nothing they could have done to make it come out differently.
c. They were not responsible for the situation, nor were they in charge of it.

And, if the family is religious, they can assure the child that the person who died is being taken care of by God and is happy.

A SENSE OF SECURITY

When something dire happens—death of a parent, divorce, burglary, etc.—children feel very insecure. Someone who has been their protector is either gone or appears inadequate to the task of keeping them safe.

Grief is the normal response of sorrow and confusion that comes from los-ing someone or something important to you. It is a typical reaction to death, divorce, job loss, a move to another town, or a loss of health. There is also an important normal emotional response in children when that loss triggers fear for their safety, security and protection. Children, for all their bravado, are fragile beings who need to be cared for and protected. They cannot really take care of themselves and they cannot survive on their own, and they know it at a very gut level.

David's father, an executive with a large manufacturing firm, had a sudden heart attack and died almost immediately. Afterwards, he heard his mother in her room sobbing and crying aloud, "Who will take care of us now?" Five-year-old David began to grow anxious that he and his mother would be thrown out of their house and have to live homeless and hungry from now on. Anxiety and depression are contagious emotions, especially for children.

When Geraldine's father divorced her mother, he was very angry and she overheard him tell her mother that he no longer loved her. Geraldine, who was only four, interpreted this to mean that her father also no longer loved her either. Children of divorce, like Geraldine, need to be reassured that they are not at fault, that they did nothing to cause the divorce, and that both parents love them as much as ever.

Raoul's home was broken into one afternoon while he was in school and both his parents were at work. Raoul, a fourth-grader, was very upset seeing his home ransacked, and for the next few nights had nightmares about his house being attacked with him inside. The one place he had counted on for feeling safe, his home, was no longer safe. Raoul needs to be reassured that everything is being done to ensure the future safety of the family home.

At times like these, children need to be reassured that, despite the traumatic life experience that happened, they are loved, safe and protected along with being cared for.

In such cases, children like Geraldine and David in the wake of the traumatic experience often fear more separation and abandonment will happen to them. Filled with separation anxiety, they may not want to leave the house and may not want the remaining parent to leave either. Such an adult may have to take time off work to be close to anxious children for a certain period. For example, the adult may have to spend much more quality time with such children.

Some children affected by a trauma that happened to a parent may develop anxiety strong enough to require professional help from a counselor or thera-pist. Children quickly pick up on feelings of parents. (Any parent can tell you that when he or she is having a bad day, that is when children will begin acting out, possibly acting out the feelings of the parent.)

After being affected by a trauma, you may notice that the child consciously avoids any activities or symbols that remind them of the original trauma or the person traumatized. The child may hide or even break a photo of the divorcing parent or a family member who died. Or the opposite may happen. The child will become preoccupied with symbols of the person traumatized and begin kissing the photo or putting it a prominent place in his/her room.

TYPICAL SIGNS IN CHILDREN
AFFECTED BY A TRAUMATIC EVENT

When a traumatic event occurs in a family, psychologists tell us that they look for some of the following typical signs that children have been strongly affected by the trauma. The child may:

Become quiet and withdrawn
Have a change in appetite
Feel and act depressed
Become jumpy and irritable
Report unexplained illnesses
Have unprovoked outbursts of anger
Become anxious or fearful
No longer interested in things that he used to find interesting
Have difficulty concentrating or completing tasks
Have trouble going to sleep or have nightmares

(These same symptoms are also characteristically found in adults affected by the trauma, too.) Psychologists tell us that most of these symptoms are normal and will usually dissipate after a time, when children are reassured that they were not responsible for the traumatic event and that they are loved, safe and will be cared for.

THE NEED FOR PROFESSIONAL COUNSELING

If some of these symptoms persist or have excessive manifestations, professional counseling is recommended. For example, after being affected by a traumatic event, it is normal for a child to become quiet and withdrawn, but if the child seems to remain estranged and totally detached from all other people, the child may need professional help.

It is also normal for a child touched by trauma to feel depressed for a time, but if the child manifests a numbness of feelings, where there is little or no affect and no sign of a lifting mood, the child may be suffering what professionals call *emotional anesthesia* and need help to overcome it.

While it is normal for a child affected by a traumatic loss to be anxious and fearful for a time, it is not normal for the child to be hyper vigilant and give exaggerated startle responses.

After a trauma happens in the family, it is typical for a child to report unexplained illnesses like stomach aches. However, it is not typical for such a child to begin making suicidal statements. And if the recurring aches and pains do not respond to household treatment and some tender loving care, seek help from a doctor.

While a child recovering from a traumatic happening may have difficulty concentrating on homework or completing household chores for a time, it is unusual for such a child, when asked what he wants to be when he grows up, not to see himself as ever having a future.

HOW DOES GRIEF DIFFER FROM DEPRESSION?

Grief is a normal experience. Shortly after a death or a loss, people—adults and children—may feel empty or numb, as if in shock. They may notice physical changes such as trembling, nausea, muscle weakness, dry mouth, shortness of breath, or trouble sleeping and eating. Emotionally, they may feel an unexplainable anger welling up at a particular person, a situation, or at nothing they can identify. They may feel guilty, saying things to themselves like, "I could have said . . ." or "I should have done . . ." or "I wish I had tried to. . ." People in grief may have strange dreams or nightmares. Socially, they may become absent-minded, avoid friends, and not want to return to work. These are the typical physical, social and emotional responses to grief. While they are normal to the grieving period, they will pass as the grief does.

Depression is something more than the feeling of grief after losing someone or something you cherish. Clinical depression is a disorder of the entire person. Though depression may begin with grief, the symptoms of grieving don't stop or lessen. They get worse and become a depression that can take over the way the child thinks and feels. The child becomes, almost, another person.

When the symptoms of grief don't subside, but grow in intensity, it is time to seek professional help. If you observe the signs of depression in an adult or a child, recommend that they see a doctor or a therapist.

SUMMARY

When children experience a crisis situation, are impacted by a traumatic event, or suffer a personal loss through death of a loved one, they begin to learn that the world they live in is not always reliable. But they also learn

Chapter Fourteen

that, when traumatic things happen, people come together to console and help each other. Adult human beings can demonstrate to children the power of the human spirit to live through and even transcend such tragedy. Those children who have such models and learn to cope effectively are more likely to build a strong sense of self-esteem, so when life deals them crushing blows, they can say to themselves, "I can get over it." And they do.

"To raise children who will be equipped to handle life's minor problems and major disasters," writes Harold S. Kusher (1981) in *When Bad Things Happen to Good People*, "always avoid destructive criticism and teach them that they are good and able people."

Chapter Fifteen

How Can You Help Yourself after a Traumatic Life Experience?

SELF HELP AS AN INTERVENTION

Any TLE employee can easily find an abundance of books, magazines and other publications written to provide guidance and support to individuals who have experienced a range of traumas. All bookstores now have a self-help section where you can select from a menu of general and specific publications. Many of these books provide insights applicable to traumatic life experiences.

One self-help publication which has applicability to a broad range of symptoms exhibited by trauma victims is: *Timeless Healing: the Power and Biology of Belief* by Herbert Benson, MD, (1996). Dr. Benson, an associate professor of medicine at Harvard Medical School, stresses the power of self-care that healthy people can provide for themselves. His book introduces a self-healing approach based on the "visceral nature of human beliefs"[1] (p.24) and our innate human impulse to turn to faith in times of illness and need. In his 30 years of practicing medicine Dr. Benson claims, "I've found no healing force more impressive or more universally accessible than the power of the individual to care for and cure him or herself."[2] (p. 22)

He writes, "I believe the ideal model for medicine is that of the three-legged stool. The stool is balanced by the appropriate application of self-care, medication, and ethical procedures"[3] (p. 23). The first leg, self-care, represents what patients can do for themselves, which includes not only nutrition and physical exercise, but also the inner development of beliefs that promote healing. Benson believes this is the most discredited and ignored aspects of health care today.

Benson postulates that invoking beliefs is not only emotionally and spiritually soothing, but also vitally important to physical wellbeing. By tapping

151

into your beliefs, which various people call "soul searching," "mulling it over," "listening to one's ear," "going inside oneself," "praying," "sleeping on it," "using your intuition" and knowing something "feels right," people tune into their internal wisdom. Benson challenges and encourages the reader, when faced with a medical decision, to ask the following question: "What feels like the right thing to do? What would I do if the choice were entirely up to me?"[4] (p. 297). He stresses letting belief play a part in the emotional recovery process by honoring your convictions and perceptions and not over relying on the medical system to give all of the answers. Benson's approach is particularly useful for TLE employees because it enables them to access their intrinsic ability to heal themselves.

Feeling Good; the New Mood Therapy by David D. Burns, M.D. (1999) is another, older book that may have wide application in understanding the emotional recovery from trauma, at least at a behavioral level. Burns proposed cognitive therapy as a self-help tool to help change your mood. By cognitive he means how you are thinking and feeling about things at a particular moment. The theory is quite simple. If you are in a depressed and anxious mood, you are most likely thinking in an illogical, negative manner and you will consequently tend to make unhelpful decisions and behave in a self-defeating manner. With some effort and practice you can train yourself to straighten your thinking patterns. Then, as the negative thinking is eliminated and is replaced by more positive patterns, your mood will lift, you will become more productive and happy again, and you will respect yourself. This transformation can be accomplished in a relatively short period of time. According to Burns, your moods are created by your own cognition or thoughts—the way you look at things and the way you interpret things. He calls this approach "fast acting."[5] (p.10) Once you replace the negative thinking, he says, you can alter any mood. This process does not, of course, eliminate the effects of the traumatic experience. It is not designed to heal the body or the short-circuited memories caused by the trauma, but it can help you shift your mood, if you have the patience and discipline to follow Burns' instructions.

Putting It All Together by Dr. Irene Kassorala (1986) is another classic with a focus on reestablishing interpersonal relationships after a trauma. An acknowledged leader in group work, Dr. Kassorla offers practical analysis, suggestions and exercises which can help a TLE individual focus and deal with the interpersonal problems they have as a result of a traumatic experience. Dr. Kassorla's focus in dealing with negative emotions within ongoing relationships is important because, TLE employees' re-entry to the workplace involves re-establishing their relationships with supervisors and co-workers.

No suggestions for self-help would be complete without mentioning Rabbi Harold S. Kushner's (1981) seminal book *When Bad Things Happen to Good People*, which has sold many millions of copies. It is filled with wise and compassionate counsel about dealing with personal tragedy. Most of us go through life, he states, with the belief that the world should be predictable, fair and understandable. Then, when something shocking happens, we feel lost. If victims are unwilling to relinquish the idea that the world is understandable, Kushner continues, they feel a desperate need to make sense of what has happened. To maintain this untenable belief, they must either find someone to blame or some deeper cause of the terrible event. Some adults even think that they deserved to have the traumatic experience, that it was an appropriate punishment for bad behavior.

Kushner takes a very different approach. He asks survivors to search for their inner strength. He wants them to recognize the energy of the human spirit that is available to everyone. In the face of a crisis, he observes, "people have a remarkable capacity to go on with their lives and mobilize their inner strength to respond positively." Evidence of this is seen in the ways people come to console each other and in their willingness to work together. Those who learn to cope effectively tend to build a strong sense of self-esteem. They develop the courage to build a new life out of the ruins of the old.

SPECIALIZED SUPPORT GROUPS

You can also join a self-help group specific to your type of traumatic experience, whether you are coping with a certain developmental disability, a chronic emotional problem, an addiction, a terminal illness, or a specific traumatic life event such as a divorce or death of a family member. Since the 1970's self-help groups have witnessed a tremendous expansion of topics, resources and people. Participants in these groups are usually individuals who share a common troubling situation and who willingly serve as helpers to assist other people, perhaps by providing information about the issue or by engaging in constructive actions with them.

Self-help groups do not provide treatment or therapy but focus on peer support and education in their area of concern. There you will meet people like yourself who have had traumatic experiences like yours. These groups are usually available at low or no cost. Counselors and therapists often suggest that their clients participate in a self-help group in order to cope more effectively with their specific problems.

NOTES

1. *Timeless Healing: the Power and Biology of Belief.* (New York, N. Y., Scribner, 1996) p. 24.

2. *Ibid.* p. 22.

3. *Ibid.* p. 23.

4. *Ibid.* p. 297.

5. *Feeling Good: The New Mood Therapy.* (New York, Harper, 1999) p. 10.

Chapter Sixteen

What Challenges Face a Facilitator?

QUESTIONS AND SENSITIVE TOPICS

It's very important to note that even before the first Study Circle session you, as the facilitator, may be challenged by questions from participants as to the importance of the topic and the need to engage in a dialogue about a sensitive topic such as trauma. Here are a few common questions and challenges that you may hear from participants of your Study Circle—and the ways I might respond to them.

"Why Do I Need To Be Here?"

It's important to point out to the participants that the subject of a TLE employee returning to the workplace involves all sectors of the organization—both employees and managerial personnel. *This must be stressed.* Everyone in the workplace either has had a trauma in their life, or is close to someone who has been through a transition that involves a trauma. This Study Circle will help participants become more sensitive to the needs of a TLE employee returning to the workplace.

"How Will I Learn?"

In a Study Circle participants all learn from each other. The active exchange of ideas and the dialogues that are shared during each session create an environment of curiosity and learning. What really needs to be learned in the Study Circle on traumatic life experiences will be learned through the sharing of experiences.

"How Will This Study Circle Help Me Do My Job Better?"

This Study Circle will make you more aware of employees when they return to the workplace after having experienced a trauma in their life. During the sessions, you will hear comments from both managers and employees. This shared experience with others and your own personal experience will enable you to understand the TLE employee better.

"As a Manager How Will This Study Circle Make Me More Effective?"

Hopefully, you will become more aware of your important role in dealing with returning TLE employees. Your role will be reflected through the eyes of the employees who will give feedback on the trauma issues that emerge, you will be able to communicate better with a returning TLE employee, and you will be able to identify and understand the stages of emotional trauma recovery as they unfold in such people.

"As an Employee, What Information Will I Take Back To the Office That Will Make My Relationships With My Colleagues Better?"

You will gain helpful information about relating to an individual who has just returned to the workplace after having experienced a trauma: How to approach that person and what to say to welcome the employee back to work appropriately.

"How Will the Organization Benefit From People Participating in This Study Circle?"

A change in attitude and behavior toward the returning TLE employee will begin happening throughout your organization. It will have an effect on employee cooperation and productivity.

CHALLENGES

Most Study Circles run smoothly because participants who volunteer for this type of Study Circle want to learn more about the topic. However, from time to time an individual's behavior or verbal comments may cause some slight disruptions during a session. Some of these behaviors can be expected around sensitive topics, as group interactions become intense with different personalities and diverse opinions surfacing. The following situations may occur during the Study Circle sessions and may need to be addressed by the facilitator.

Situation: The employee in the Study Circle does not want to talk or share personal experiences.

Response: Don't make the employee feel uncomfortable. If a participant does not want to share, the facilitator simply moves on with the discussion or asks another participant to talk about his or her experience. A non-judgmental approach is best in this situation, since the resistant participant may have good reasons for not discussing certain personal points.

Situation: A participant consistently dominates, interrupts or monopolizes the session with his experiences and stories.

Response: Sometimes in groups you encounter individuals who have a great need to talk, thus preventing other people from getting their share of group time. As a session progresses, the group will usually become less tolerant of such an individual who always wants to talk. A person who exhibits this type of behavior needs to be gently challenged to look at the effects of their behavior. You, as the facilitator, can gently confront the person and say, "Let's focus on another person's experience for awhile." Or, you may approach the participant by saying something like: "Sally, you appear to share easily. I notice you typically identify with most of the problems that have been raised in the group. Is there anything special that you want us to know about you? Otherwise, there are others who would like to speak." This intervention will give Sally an opportunity to gracefully stop. If she continues to monopolize the session, the facilitator can talk with her privately during a break.

Situation: Suppose a participant begins to cry during a session, as can be expected in the second session when persons reconstruct their trauma experiences.

Response: Allow the participant to cry. Comfort the participant yourself, either verbally or by a gentle touch, if someone else in the group has not already done so, and assure him that it is okay to cry/weep. Continue on with the Study Circle.

Situation: Suppose a participant in the Study Circle starts criticizing or blaming other participants as they tell their story, thereby creating a disruption in the group.

Response: Participants should be advised at the beginning of the Study Circle that this is a learning experience for everyone and it's important to maintain a learning environment. If a person does not heed this advice, then the facilitator might want to have a private conversation with the participant after the session.

DIFFICULT QUESTIONS

If a participant asks the facilitator a question to which the facilitator does not know the answer, the facilitator should acknowledge the question and promise to find the answer and get back to them at a specific time, e.g., in an hour, or at the next session.

I recall once that a participant asked me about some form of therapy for traumatized people he had heard was being used on an employee. I had never heard of this therapeutic intervention, told him so, and promised to find out about it and report back to the group. I did so, and in my research found many new approaches that psychologists and psychiatrists were using to understand the emotional recovery in traumatized patients. I found my research so interesting that I thought readers of this book my like to know about them too. I reported on some of these in Chapter 6 "What Psychology Tell Us About Trauma."

Also, many times in a well-planned session something may go wrong and there may be some time constraints that may keep the discussion from moving forward. The session may have been late getting started, the discussion may get sidetracked from the topic for a time, someone in the group may get emotionally upset recalling a traumatic experience and may need to be cared for, or you may have a group where everyone wants to share their stories and each one's story is quite long and involved.

The facilitator may bring the issue of a lack of time to the group's attention and the content they need to cover. Then, the facilitator adjusts by quickly moving through certain portions of the discussion, watching the clock to ensure having an appropriate amount of time for processing the session,

RESISTANT PARTICIPANTS

If an organization makes the Study Circle a requirement for managers and employees, some employees may not want to participate because they may think it is an inconvenience, imposition, invasion of their privacy or robbing them of their work or lunch time. If this happens, there may be some questions about and resistance to participating.

Here are some common forms of resistance:

- I really don't want to be here, I feel this is just a waste of my time.
- We have been okay dealing with this problem before in our office. How are you going to make things easier for me by requiring me to attend a Study Circle?

- Do I have to change my whole personality to take care of this returning TLE employee? I'd rather not deal with him.
- Does this mean that I won't have to go to the Employee Assistance Program (EAP) when I have a problem?

Here are some suggested ways to respond:
- If the participant is adamant about not wanting to attend, perhaps you can speak to his supervisor and have him excused. The best participants are those who attend willingly. A few angry and resentful participants can ruin a Study Circle.
- If the participant is merely hedging about attending the sessions, he or she may simply need some encouragement, such as, "Every participant has said how helpful and useful the sessions were. You'd probably enjoy being part of the group."
- Suggest to the participant to talk to a colleague who has participated in Study Circle to get some feedback as to the nature of the dialogue and interaction.

FACILITATOR EXPECTATIONS

Most of my Study Circle groups consist of managers and employees with no specific interpersonal skill base; they come only because of availability and referral. Invariably, their chemistry is excellent. They get along exceptionally well and freely share their experiences with each other. These groups seem also to enjoy light humor and no one seems to feel a need to up-stage another participant.

After facilitating a number of these Study circles on managing workplace trauma, I began to have certain expectations of the Study Circle process. For example, I expected the group to develop a trusting cohesion, if not during the first session, certainly by the second. Sometimes, my expectations were not fulfilled.

I once had a group of participants most of whom happened to be experts in their fields: one was an Alternative Dispute Resolution expert, two were lawyers, two were Labor-Relations executives, two were workshop leaders and trainers, and two were Human Resource managers. During pre-Study Circle interviews, each of these participants shared not only their trauma stories and their experiences, but also information about their careers and life experiences. But during the Study Circle itself they remained silent about their personal traumas.

When the actual sessions began, I fully expected that because these individuals were seasoned managers—even though some knew each other, and some did not—they would come together as a group with excellent group dynamics. This did not happen.

Instead, no chemistry seemed to develop in the group. Except for a very few, and hesitantly, they did not share their trauma experiences publicly in the group, even though privately they had told me about them in great detail. This was a puzzling situation. What I soon realized was that this group of experts were used to being presenters and team leaders, not participants. They were used to being up front, on stage. They saw themselves as the ones expected to have the answers, to give advice and direction to others. They were not used to revealing themselves as vulnerable, especially in front of each other. And they seemed unwilling to change their public image.

The more ordinary employees in the group were swayed and perhaps awed by these experts, and so hesitated to offer opinions or disagree. Because the experts were all seen as having power in their career roles, they were able to influence the others to agree on what managerial skills were needed in dealing with a returning TLE employee.

These experts seemed most concerned with teaching the other participants and promoting the value of listening skills. Over and over, they pointed out how managers needed to be trained and skilled in good communication and active listening skills, but, ironically, as representatives of these skills, they did not walk their talk.

Although they were all certified as experts in group process, their technical skills did not appear to help them in the Study Circle sessions. Their skills seemed to inhibit them from opening up and sharing their own life and trauma experiences. It looked like these same people were rather posturing and pontificating during the sessions, as one employee pointed out. Their advice in the group was directed outward and not inward toward themselves.

I wonder whether these experts would be able to create a welcome environment for a returning TLE employee, since they were unable to do it among the group in the Study Circle sessions.

In cases like these, as a facilitator it is well to keep in mind some important elements for facilitating according to Roger M. Schwarz (1994) in his book *The Skilled Facilitator*. They are as follows:

a. The whole group is the facilitator's client; the facilitator is not a group member and cannot focus all the groups' attention on certain members at the expense of others.
b. The main task of the facilitator is to increase group effectiveness. Here, both content and process are important.

c. Facilitators must remain neutral, and allow the group to solve their problems.

Realizing that cohesion was not happening after the first session with this group, I was not sure what to do. So I simply continued following the Study Circle process and, even though the group never did develop a strong cohesion, everyone managed to profit much from the sessions. Evaluations assured me that the Study Circle had been useful and practical for just about everyone. But because these managers refused to share their stories and life experiences during the second and last sessions, I felt this Study Circle provided a poorer learning experience for that group, especially since I knew the richness of all their stories from the pre-Study Circle interviews.

I also realized it is important for the facilitator to be aware that the kinds of individuals recruited for the sessions will make a difference in the quality and tone of the Study Circle. For example, if you recruit a group all of whom are engineers, their technical expertise may bias their views on how to approach a returning TLE employee. A similar biased result may occur if you find yourself facilitating a group all of whom are counselors or group-process-oriented people.

Another important observation concerns self-disclosure. The closest and most meaningful relationships that humans enjoy involve self-disclosure. Self-disclosure is not meant to make people feel more separate or alone, it is meant to do the opposite. It frequently brings co-workers and friends closer. During the second session in the group with all the experts I asked an employee in the group to tell her trauma story. This was a conscious decision on my part to try to create more sharing, to prime the pump, as it were. It worked, but only to get the other employees in the group to tell their stories; the experts did not follow suit.

Appendix

Study Circle Handouts

THE ROLE OF THE PARTICIPANT

The participants in a Study Circle are the most important element of a Study Circle. Their commitment, eagerness and interest help make the Study Circle a success.

An important remember to know about the Study Circle is that textual material does not have to be memorized and participants do not have to learn a lot of facts. Rather encourage participants to focus on the interaction with each other and thereby gain a deep understanding of the topic through listening to their experience. The process—an open democratic dialogue with colleagues—is an important part of this experience.

The following points adapted from *The Study Circle Handbook: A manual for Study Circle Discussion Leaders, Organizers and Participants.* (1993) will assist those participating in a Study Circle:

1. Make a commitment to attend all Study Circle sessions. Each Study Circle creates its own culture and getting to know the people with whom who you will spend this time is part of the ongoing learning experience of a Study Circle.
2. Communicate your thoughts and feelings to others. Share your perceptions and suggestions with the group and ask for clarification of others' experiences when issues are not clear. Even though you may feel alone in your experience, you may be helping the group by sharing it.
3. Keep the discussion focused. Try not to bring in other ideas or topics that have no relevance to what is being discussed in your Study Circle. But don't hesitate to bring in relevant points for discussion.

4. Speak to the group. When addressing your remarks, address the entire group, not just the leader/facilitator. Feel free to engage directly in dialogue with other participants; everyone learns from interactions among the group members.

5. Listen to others. Give everyone a chance to speak and be heard. If you have a question for a group member, don't hesitate to ask the person to elaborate on a specific point. Also, be aware that some people may not be as assertive as others and may need time to come forward with their thoughts.

6. Speak up. Don't hesitate to engage in the Study Circle discussion; however, be sensitive that you do not monopolize the discussion. Encourage others to participate and express their points of view.

7. Don't withdraw from the group. Each person in the Study Circle brings unique skills and experiences to the topic. It's important to draw on these experiences during the Study Circle sessions. Not participating keeps the whole group from learning what you know.

8. Friendly disagreement. Conflict among participants is not discouraged. We all learn when people disagree and share their opinions with the group. Ideas can be challenged and individuals can be the catalyst in the group for bringing up new ideas. However, it is important that group emotions not get out of hand.

9. Humor. Your personality is key is the group participation. If humor can be used to lighten up a session, it is encouraged. Be aware of your body language and the body language of others.

10. Keep an open mind. Your participation is appreciated when you come to each Study Circle with an open mind to learning and engaging others. Don't hesitate to engage others in a dialogue about points that may need clarification or an idea that you may want to discuss.

11. Evaluate critical faculties. Think about what is being said in the sessions. It's important for you to keep a critical eye on statements made by authors of readings, the leader/facilitator, or other participants. Don't allow yourself to be intimidated by false assertions.

12. Understand the people who you may disagree with you. It's important to understand another person's point of view, before outwardly criticizing that individual. They usually have a very good reason why they do not see a situation the same way you do. If you show empathy and understanding, many times your point of view will be heard with a different ear.

References

Aldrin, B. 2009. *Magnificent Desolation*. New York: Harmony Books.

Allen, Jon G. 1995. *Coping with trauma: A guide to self-understanding*. Washington, D.C.: American Psychiatric Press, Inc.

———. 1993. The Study Circle Handbook: A manual for Study Circle Discussion Leaders, Organizers and Participants. Pomfret, Connecticut: Topsfield Foundation Inc.

———. 1990. Guidelines for rape victims. American College of Obstetricians and Gynecologists. Washington, D.C.

Attig, Thomas.1996. *How we grieve: relearning the world*. New York: Oxford University Press.

Bahls, C. 2000. Program helps hospitals deal with rape cases. *Healtheon: WebMD Medical News*.

Bart, P. 1975. *Unalienating abortion, demystifying depressing, and restoring rape victims*. Paper presented at the 128th annual convention of the American Psychiatric Association, in Anaheim, Calif.

Bass, Ellen, and Laura Davis. 1988. *The courage to heal*. New York: Harper Perennial.

Bates, J.A. 2000. Is the silence broken? Thirty years after rape crisis centers, *Healtheon: WebMD Medical News*.

Bathrop, R.W. 1977. *Depressed Lymphocyte function after bereavement*. Lancet. April 15, 1977: 834-36.

Benson, Herbert. 1996. *Timeless healing: The power and biology of belief*. New York: Scribner.

Bergmann, U. 2000. *Exploring the role of the cerebellum in Eye Movement and Desensization andRe processing*. Paper presented at the Eye Movement and Desensization and Reprocessing International Conference, in Toronto, Ontario.

Bloom, Sandra. 1997. *Creating sanctuary: Toward an evolution of sane societies*. New York: Routledge.

Bowlby, John. 1980.*Attachment and Loss*, vols I-III, New York: Basic Books.

Brooks, Jane. 1999. *Midlife orphan: Facing life's changes now that your parents are gone*. New York: Berkley Books.

Braverman, Mark, and Susan Braverman. 1994. Seeking solutions to violence on the job. *USA Today Magazine*, May.

Bridges, William. 1994. Job shift: How to prosper in a workplace without jobs. New York: Addison-Wesley Publishing Co.

Burns, David. 1999. *Feeling Good: The New Mood Therapy*. New York: Harper Collins Publishers.

Caffarella, Rosemary, and Sharon Merriam. 1991. *Learning in adulthood*. San Francisco: Jossey Bass Publishers.

Carkhuff, Robert. 1993. *The art of healing*. Amherst, MA: Human Resources Development Press.

Charles, Sara, and Kennedy, Eugene. 1990. *On becoming a counselor: A basic guide for non-professionals*. NewYork: Crossroad Publishing Co.

Charles-Edwards, David. 2005. *Handling death and bereavement at work*. New York: Routledge Taylor and Francis Group.

Christensen, Erik. 1983. Study circles: Learning in small groups. *Journal of Specialists in Group Work*: 211-217.

Corey, Gerald, and Marianne Corey. 1999. *Groups: Process and Practice*. New York: Brook Cole Publishing Co.

Covey, Stephen. 2003. *The 7 Habits of Highly Effective People*. New York: Simon & Schuster.

Davidson-Nielson, Marianne, and Nini Leeck. 1993. *Healing pain: Attachment, loss and grief therapy*. New York: Routledge.

Dayton, Tian. 2000. *Trauma and addiction: Ending the cycle of pain through emotional literacy*. Deerfield Beach, Florida: Health Communications, Inc.

Dutton, Jane. 2003. *Energize Your Workplace: How to create and sustain high-quality connections at work*. San Francisco: Jossey-Bass.

Egendorg, Arthur. 1985. *Healing from the war-trauma and transformation after Vietnam*. Boston: Shambhala Publications.

Engel, George. 1961. Is Grief a Disease: A Challenge for Medical Research. *Psychosomatic Medicine* 23: 18-27.

Epstein, Fred, and Joshua Horowitz. 2003. *If I get to five: What children teach us teach us about courage and character*. New York: Henry Holt & Co.

Everstine, Diane and Louis Everstine. 1983. *People in Crisis and Trauma: Strategic Therapeutic Interventions*. New York: Penguin Books.

Fanos, Joanna. 1996. *Sibling Loss*. Mahwah, New Jersey. Lawrence Erlbaum Associates Publishers.

Foa, Eda, and Barbara Rothbaum. 1998. *Treating the Trauma of Rape: Cognitive Therapy for PTSD*. NewYork: Guilford Press.

Frost, Peter J. 2003. *Toxic Emotions at Work: How compassionate managers handle pain and conflict*. Boston, Massachusetts: Harvard Business School Press.

Gendlin, Eugene. 1978. *Focusing*. New York: Bantam Dell Publishing Group.

Golden, Tom. 1996. *Swallowed by a snake: The gift of the masculine side of healing*. Gaithersburg, Maryland. Glassner, Barry. 1994. *Career Crash: The New Crisis and Who Survives*. New York: Simon & Schuster.

Goldman, Linda. 2005. *Raising our children to be resilient: A guide to helping children cope with trauma in today's world.* New York: Brunner-Routledge.

Gould, Joseph Edward. 1961. *The Chatauqua Movement: An episode in the continuing American revolution.* New York: State University of New York.

Groopman, Jerome. 2004. *The anatomy of hope: How people prevail in the face of illness.* New York: Random House.

Herman, Judith Lewis. 1992. *Trauma and recovery.* New York: Harper Collins. Horowitz, Mardi. 1986. *Stress response* syndromes. Northvale, New Jersey: Jason Aronson.

Janoff, Bonnie. 1993. *Shattered Assumptions.* New York: The Free Press.

Jeffreys, Shep. 1995. *Coping with Workplace Grief: Dealing with loss, trauma, and change.* Boston, Thomson Course Technology.

Jeffreys, Shep. 2005. *Helping grieving people when tears are not enough: A handbook for care providers.* New York: Brunner-Routledge.

Kassorla, Irene. 1986. *How to be a total person: Putting it all together.* New York: Warner Press.

Khoshaba, Deborah, and Maddi, Salvatore. 2005. *Resilience at work: How to Succeed No Matter What Life Throws at You.* New York: American Management Association.

Kubler-Ross, Elizabeth. 1969. *On death and dying.* New York: Macmillan.

Kurland, Norman. 1982. The Scandinavian study circle: An idea for the U.S. *The college board review*: 24-30.

Kushner, Harold. 1990. *When Bad Things Happen to Good People.* New York: Anchor Books.

Levine, Peter. 1997. *Waking the Tiger: Healing trauma.* Berkeley, California: North Atlantic Books.

Lumsden, Gay, and Tonyald Lumsden. 1992. *Communications in Groups and Teams: Shared Leadership.* New York: Wadsworth Publishing Co.

Mantell, Michael. 1994. *Ticking Bombs: Defusing Violence in the Workplace.* New York: Irwin Professional Publishing.

Matsakis, Aphrodite. 1998. *Trust after trauma: A guide to relationships for survivors and those who love them.* Oakland, California: New Harbinger Publications, Inc.

Matsakis, Aphrodite. 1996. *I can't get over it: A handbook for trauma survivors.* Oakland, California: New Harbinger Publications, Inc.

Miller, Benjamin and Claire Keane. 2000. Miller-Keane Medical Dictionary, *Healtheon: WebMD Medical News.*

Montada, Leo Sigrun Heide-Flipp, and Melvin Lerner. 1992. *Life crisis and experiences of loss in adulthood.* Hillsdale, New Jersey: Lawrence Erlbaum Associates.

Nadeau, Janet. 1998. *Families making sense of death.* London: Sage Publications.

Neimeyer, Robert. 1998. *Lessons of loss: A guide to coping.* New York: The McGraw Hill Companies, Inc.

Noer, David. 1993. *Healing the wounds: Overcoming the trauma of layoffs and revitalizing downsized organizations.* San Francisco: Jossey Bass Publishers.

Oliver, Leonard. 1987. *Study Circles coming together for personal growth and social change.* Washington, D. C.: Seven Locks Press.

Oliver, Leonard. 1995. Is the United States ready for a study circle movement? *Adult Education.* March/April: 14-19.

Oliver, Leonard. 1990. Study Circles: A new life for an old idea. *Advocacy*. November: 20-22.

Osborne, Katie. 1982. Study circles: Personal professional fulfillment for employees. *Management Review*. June: 37-42. 1982.

Parnell, Laurel. 1997. *Transforming trauma: EMDR*. New York: W.W. Norton & Co.

Perlman, Helen Harris. 1983. *Relationship: The heart of helping people*. Chicago: The University of Chicago Press.

Prend, Ashley Davis. 1997. *Transcending loss: Understanding the lifelong impact of grief and how to make it meaningful*. New York: Berkley Books.

Rosenbloom, Dena, and Mary Beth Williams. 1999. *Life after trauma: A workbook for healing*. New York: The Guilford Press.

Rothbaum, Barbara, and Eda Foa, David Riggs, Tamera Murdoch and W. Walsh. 1992. A prospective examination of post-traumatic stress disorder in rape victims. *Journal of Traumatic Stress,* 5: 455-475.

Sanders, Catherine. 1999. *Grief: The mourning after, dealing with adult bereavement*. New York: John Wiley & Sons, Inc.

Sanders, Catherine. 1992. *Surviving grief: and learning to live again*. New York: John Wiley & Sons, Inc.

Sargent, W. and E. Slater. 1940. Acute war neuroses. *Lancet, ii*: 1-2.

Schore, Allan. 2000. Traumatic attachment and the development of the right brain. Paper given at the EMDR International Conference, Toronto, Ontario.

Seyle, Hans. 1956. *The stress of life*. New York: McGraw-Hill Companies. Schneider, John. 1984. *Stress, loss and grief*. Baltimore, Maryland: University Park Press.

Shapiro, Francine. 1995. *Eye movement desensitization and reprocessing: Basic principles, and* procedures. New York: Guilford Press.

Slaby, Andrew. 1989. *Aftershock: Surviving the delayed effects of trauma, crisis and loss:* New York, New York: Villard.

Spiegel, D. 1989. Hypnosis in the treatment of victims of sexual abuse. *Psychiatric Clinics of North America 12*: 295-305.

Stubblefield, Harold, and Patrick Keane. 1994. *Adult education in the American experience: From the colonial period to the present*. San Francisco: Jossey-Bass Publishers.

Suinn, Richard, and R. Weigel. 1974. *The innovative therapy: Critical and creative contributions*. New York: Harper & Row.

Tatelbaum, Judy. 1980. *The courage to grieve: Creative living, recovery and growth through grief*. New York: Harper & Row.

Tedeschi, Richard, and Lawrence Calhoun. 1995. *Trauma and transformation: Growing in the aftermath of suffering*. London: Sage Publications.

Trozzi, Maria, and and Kathy Massimi. 1999. *Talking to children about loss: Words strategies, and wisdom to help children cope with death, divorce, and other difficult times*. New York: Berkley Publishing Group.

Ulman, Richard, and Doris Brothers. 1988. *The shattered self: A psychoanalytic study of trauma*. Hillsdale, New Jersey: The Analytic Press.

van der Kolk, Bessel, Helene Boyd, John Krystal, and Mark Greenberg. 1985. Inescapable shock, neurotransmitters and addition to trauma: Towards a psychobiology of post-traumatic stress. *Biological Psychiatry,* 20: 314-325.

Van der Kolk, Bessel. 2000. Trauma, attachment, and the body. Paper given at the EMDR International Conference, Toronto, Ontario.

ver Ellen, P. & van Kammen, D.P. 1990. The biological findings in post-traumatic stress disorder: A review. *Journal of Applied Social Psychology* 20, 21: 1789-1821.

Viorst, Judith. 1986. *Necessary losses.* New York: Simon & Schuster. Wilson, John. 2006. *The posttraumatic self: Restoring meaning and wholeness to personality.* New York: Routledge Taylor & Francis Group.

Worden, J. William. 1991. *Grief counseling and grief therapy: A handbook for the Mental Health Practitioner.* New York: The Springer Company.

Wolfelt, Alan. 2005. *Healing grief at work: 100 practical ideas after your workplace is touched by loss.* Fort Collins, Colorado: Companion.

Yalom, Irvin. 1995. *The theory and practice of group psychotherapy.* New York: Basic Books.

Zunin, Leonard, and Hilary Stanton Zunin. 1991. *The art of condolence: What to write, what to say, what to do at a time of* loss. New York: Harper Collins Publishers.

Breinigsville, PA USA
15 April 2010
236250BV00001B/1/P